THEOLOGY OF A CLASSLESS SOCIETY

THEOLOGY OF A CLASSLESS SOCIETY

by

GEEVARGHESE MAR OSTHATHIOS

*Metropolitan of the Orthodox Syrian Church
in Kerala, South India*

ORBIS BOOKS
Maryknoll, New York 10545

The Catholic Foreign Mission Society of America (Maryknoll) recruits and trains people for overseas missionary service. Through Orbis Books Maryknoll aims to foster the international dialogue that is essential to mission. The books published, however, reflect the opinions of their authors and are not meant to represent the official position of the society.

Library of Congress Cataloging in Publication Data

Osthathios, Geevarghese, Metropolitan, 1918-
    Theology of a classless society.

    1. Sociology, Christian.   2. Social classes—
Moral and religious aspects.   I. Title.
BT738.O77   1980   261.8'345   79-27013
ISBN 0-88344-500-X

First published by Lutterworth Press, Luke House, Farnham Road, Guildford, Surrey, England

Copyright © 1979 by Geevarghese Mar Osthathios

U.S. edition 1980 by Orbis Books, Maryknoll, NY 10545

Filmset in Great Britain; printed and bound in the United States of America

CONTENTS

THE AUTHOR

His Grace Geevarghese Mar Osthathios (59) took his B.D. from Leonard Theological College, Jabalpur, India, M.A. from Drew University, Madison, New Jersey and STM from Union Theological Seminary, New York, where he studied under Reinhold Niebuhr, Paul Tillich and Georges Florovsky. He has been teaching Theology and Ethics at the Orthodox Theological Seminary for the past 25 years. He was consecrated a Metropolitan on 16th February 1975, and is still teaching part time at the Seminary. Most of his books are in Malayalam, his mother tongue. His books in English include an outline on Christology entitled, *My Lord and My God, New Life in an Old Church,* and *Talks to Modern Youth.*

He was a delegate to the World Youth Assembly in Kottayam 1952, the first assembly of the East Asia Christian Conference in Kuala Lumpur 1959, Commission on World Mission and Evangelism Assembly at Bangkok 1973, and was an Adviser at the Fifth Assembly of the World Council of Churches at Nairobi 1975. He is a member of the Faith and Order Commission of the World Council of Churches and attended its meeting at Accra in 1974. He has also participated in the 3 Vienna Consultations between Oriental Orthodox and Roman Catholic theologians sponsored by the Pro-Oriente Foundation.

He has travelled widely in India and abroad as a preacher and is regarded by his countrymen as a modern prophet of social justice. He is the founder of St. Paul's Wyoming Gospel Hall, Mavelikara, and St. Paul's Children's Home, Puthupady. He has also founded humanitarian projects like Sick Aid Foundation, Marriage Assistance Foundation, House Building Aid Fund and Scholarship Loan Fund.

FOREWORD

The speeches and writings of Geevarghese Mar Osthathios, a shepherd of the Orthodox Church in Kerala, India, have continued to express the anguish felt by a sensitive soul at the contradiction between the spirit of fellowship in Christ which the church preaches and the caste and class structure which the church supports. He has also expressed his concern for the poor in a number of humanitarian projects. In this book he digs into the heritage of orthodox theology and the Bible to build up his case for a social expression of the spirit of fellowship in the modern world. He calls it the classless society, the word class not being used in any technical economic sense, but defined as any division in society which makes for exploitation and inequality between fellow human beings and destroys brotherly communion. He also indicates some of the implications of Christian commitment to fellowship in the structure of the life and mission of the church itself. In fact one may say that Mar Osthathios is here primarily concerned not with orthodoxy but with orthopraxis, the working out of the spirit of orthodoxy in contemporary society.

Theology of a Classless Society provides an ideology and a programme for a social democratic transformation of our class-ridden society, informed by the Christian evangelical concern for justice. Mar Osthathios is in the same tradition of the prophetic ministry as Amos of old. Even if it is a voice crying in the wilderness as that of John the Baptist, it is a voice that must be heard in our contemporary world. It has a message not only to India, but to the whole world. It is a relevant and challenging book and I hope it will receive the attention it deserves.

M. M. Thomas

INTRODUCTION

Is the title *Theology of a Classless Society* one more new theology like Black Theology, Liberation Theology, Death of God Theology etc., which according to many are all passing fashions? Is there anything new in the *Theology of a Classless Society* except the hated communism? Why not use a title other than 'classless society' which has Marxian overtones? I hope the reader will have answers for all such initial apprehensions when he or she reads the book with an open mind.

It was the Faith and Order Meeting in Ghana in 1974 which inspired me to write a book with such a title, especially because my suggestion to the plenary session there to launch such a study fell on deaf ears. There is hardly anything new in the book except the trinitarian basis for social justice, collegiality of hierarchy, unity of the church and unity of mankind, sustainable and participatory society, limits to growth debate, proletarian and simpler life-style etc., of which we all read in the religious and secular press. The centrality of the doctrine of Trinity is behind every chapter of the book. Western theologians are likely to charge me with tritheism in taking the analogy of a nuclear family to explain the mystery of Trinity. Eastern theologians may also ask me whether the Fathers of the church have spoken of the Holy Spirit as Mother. The Fathers were emphatic on the unknowability of the essence of God and of the inexpressibility of the mystery of Trinity to which I also subscribe. No analogy from the created order can exhaust the mystery of Godhead. But we speak of the adorable lest we be silent about the ultimate truth we know to be true by the self revelation of God in Christ.

My thesis is that 'God is love' means that God is Trinity and that love in its ultimacy is co-equal, co-eternal, co-essential as the Blessed Trinity. There is no collegial unit in history which can express the collegiality, unity, co-equality and classlessness like a nuclear family and so I am using that analogy,

11

granting that there is some danger of emphasizing the threeness by many readers without an equal stress on singularity and unity. To me the nuclear family is a tremendous singularity holding father, mother and child in perfect solidarity in spite of the distinctions. Therefore, my plea is that we should understand creation in the image of God as triune image of the eternal love in eternal action in his very being. Trinity is the perfection of love. Threeness is for the circular motion of love and unity is the ontological effect of love and both are inseparable as in a perfect family on earth.

We may say that God is one and at the same time a classless society of perfect equality, which makes him a co-being, one in three and three in one. The primacy of the Father is that of *primus inter pares* (first among equals) and such should be the primacy of the Pope or of the Patriarch or of the Archbishop in Synod. The classless society of the state, nation or world must also be modelled according to the Holy Trinity if perfection is the goal. Trinity is the key that would unlock many riddles that baffle thinkers of our day such as authority and freedom, individuality and sociality, equality and distinction.

It seems to me that any true Christian theology is a theology of a classless society. Can there be any theological justification for a class structured society in which we are all caught up and demonized today? Even the world outside the church is speaking about the need of egalitarianism, socialism, social justice, world brotherhood, international economic order, world government etc., which are all squarely based on Christian theology, rightly understood. Our animosity to the title, if any, may not be because of its communistic overtones, but because we do not want to part with the undue privileges we have in the first class compartment in which many of us travel, when the majority of humanity is starving in the third class compartment of the space ship called the earth. We do not want to be reminded of the naked truth that we are all robbers who have robbed both God and our fellowmen to remain in the luxurious upper class. We do not want to recognize the simple Christian teaching that everything visible and invisible belongs to God the creator-Father and is intended for all his children and not for the privileged few who have made the majority to sweat for the minority.

12

Many would discard the contentions of the book as idealistic and abstract, not knowing that God is already at work in the world to create a classless society. The observation of Mao Tse-tung in 'On Practice' is relevant here: 'Fully to reflect a thing in its totality, to reflect its essence, to reflect its inherent laws, it is necessary through the exercise of thought to reconstruct the data of sense perception; discarding the dross and selecting the essential; . . . in order to form a system on concepts and theories it is necessary to make a leap from perceptual to rational knowledge.'[1] No one, I hope, will contend that theology of a classless society is irrational. It is based on the Scriptures and on God-given reason as every sound theology is. It is what the Spirit says to the churches in these latter days. I hope some abler person would say these things in a better way.

Our unwillingness to part with private property is because it is the symbol of power and we do not want to be powerless. But we must remember that we live in a world where vote is power, education is power, knowledge is power, organization is power, as Dr. C. T. Kurian points out. 'Even granting that ownership is the main and crucial base of power, it seems neither possible nor necessary to insist that power arises solely from ownership of resources.'[2] We Christians ought to realize the power of the cross to transform the world and be satisfied with the power that others also have, like the vote, instead of clinging on to special power for ourselves. As I uphold the democratic system in which the opposition party is a necessity, I believe that the people should have the power of the vote to overthrow corrupted power which spoils the classless unity of the people and the sharing of privileges for all. I consider the atheism of communism as a passing phenomenon, for God is not an option that man may accept or reject; he is the very Ground of Being (Tillich) without whom man cannot live as man for long. When the people take counsel against the Lord and his anointed, 'he who sits in the heavens laughs' (Psa. 2). The bane of communism is its one party system which thwarts opposition rather than its materialism which also is a half-truth which will be corrected. It is the power of the vote that must be reserved for the people so that they can punish the power of the oligarchy or bureaucracy which might be at the helm of affairs, by making them powerless through the ballot box. The classless society envisaged in this book, therefore, is not what Marx taught, but a democratic socialism with nationalization of the means of production, and work and just wages for all. The opposition party is to be a corrective to the party in power and not a means to usher in capitalism or feudalism which will take away the classlessness of the people. Equality of opportunity for all the people of all the world is the ideal and not the creation of an affluent class on the one hand and the exploited poor class on the other. A two–party system is not impossible in a classless egalitarian society, if both the parties are committed to socialism and welfare of all.

Those brought up in the capitalistic system may consider the book as too radical to deserve attention. Having lived in the United States of America for 3 years and visited Soviet Russia on 3 occasions I am not a stranger to the practical applications of capitalism and socialism. India with its acute poverty has conditioned my thinking more than the west or the east. If the church is to be true to the Lord and to the inner ethos of Christianity, she must accept and teach a theology of a classless society, though she may not be in total agreement with the details of this book. If more competent theologians take up the theme and carry it further, I shall be grateful.

May I put on record my appreciation of the services of my friend Dr. M. M. Thomas for the fine foreword he has written.

'He who has an ear, let him hear what the Spirit says to the churches.'

Geevarghese Mar Osthathios

1
THE QUEST FOR A
CLASSLESS SOCIETY

The Quest of the Secular World

Morarji Desai, the Prime Minister of India, in his first broadcast to the nation, declared, 'We have to create a culture that is egalitarian, not exploitative. And we can no more tolerate dual societies of rich and poor, city and village. We must not think of town and country as separate and rival entities or cultures, but as integrated and independent settlements within finite regions.'[3] Over a 100 years ago, Karl Marx said in item 9 of the 'generally applicable measures' of the Manifesto of the Communist Party published in 1848, that there should be a combination of agriculture with manufacturing industries and a gradual abolition of the distinction between town and country by a more equable distribution of population over the country.[4] Desai and Marx are not of the same school of thought, but on the question of an egalitarian society there is no difference of opinion.

There is a new quest for a world of peace and justice in the public pronouncements of all leaders and thinkers of our time, though there is a no concentrated action to achieve it. Jimmy Carter, the President of the United States of America, expressed this sentiment in his address to the United Nations on 17th March 1977. 'I see a hopeful world, a world dominated by increasing demands for basic freedom, for fundamental rights, for higher standards of human existence. We are eager to take part in the shaping of this world . . .' However he went on to recognize that 'every headline reminds us of bitter divisions of national hostilities, of territorial conflicts, of ideological competitions . . . Poverty and inequality are of such monumental scope that it will take decades of deliberate and determined effort even to improve the situation'. One of his aims was a persistent effort 'to help build a better and more co-operative international economic system and to work with potential adversaries as well as with our friends to advance the cause of human rights'. He also wanted to 'participate in moulding a global economic system which will bring greater prosperity to the people of all countries'.[5]

A. B.Vajpayee, India's Minister for External Affairs, was speaking on behalf of all the developing countries when he declared in a recorded and televised message at Belgrade on 18th April 1977 that the industrialized countries should understand that it was in their own interest to have a more equitable development all over the world. 'If non-aligned nations, are steadfast enough and do all they can in establishing a more equitable development of the world in general, they will be successful.'[6] Shridath Ramphal, Secretary General of the British Commonwealth, in Washington on 23rd April 1977, called upon the United States to join in an international economic system to help the poor countries. He said that 'by 1985 the increase in per capita incomes over 1965 incomes for the poorest group of nations would be $50 compared to $3,900 for the richest countries. The non oil developing countries could have balance of payments deficits reaching 50 billion dollars.' He called for an entire restructuring of trade and international financial arrangements to improve the lot of the poor nations.[7]

The Quest of Modern Theologies

The quest for a classless society is not limited to the secular world or to Marxism. Modern theological movements, whether Liberation Theology or Black Theology or Death of God Theology, without exception are quests for a theology of a classless society.

Frederick Herzog [8] has pointed out that there can be no systematic theology in North America today without an analysis of Marx. Theology that doesn't take the poor into account from the outset is not Christian theology. He then goes on to quote from a previous article on 'Third World

16

Theology, Fourth World Liberation'. 'Once considered exotic and fanciful, liberation theologies now have a good chance of becoming the way ahead for theology in the next century—if only they can manage to be true to the aspirations of the oppressed and to the reality of the beyond in their midst.' The reference to Liberation Theology is equally applicable to the theology of a classless society dealt with in this book. 'To put it somewhat rashly: Liberation Theology in the United States did not emerge because some people were looking in more kindly fashion on the poor, but because the poor were looking in more unkindly fashion on some people. In a new encounter with the Bible, the poor crossed the threshold of the theological consciousness. God's claim in the poor Christ was felt anew. The experience was not triggered by the kindly sentiments of do-gooder white theologians. Rather, 'objective' claims made on us by God and by the poor on the margins of society turned us around . . . The relationship between the poor and the rich is one dimension among others, but one that has been widely overlooked in Protestant theology.'

The task of theology is to reinterpret the contents of the revealed and permanent dogma to the particular needs of each age. There is no dogma more permanent for a Christian understanding of God than the dogma of Holy Trinity. God wants us to look into this venerable dogma again, not as an article of belief, but as one of praxis. Hence God is himself guiding the thinking of theologians as well as of other people to evolve a theology of a classless society, whether we call it Liberation Theology or the Pedagogy of the Oppressed or by some other name. To quote Dr. Herzog again, 'In praxis empowered by the New Testament, it is not we who create theology, but God of the poor. This is the way Christianity began. This is the way it still begins, making us immerse ourselves in history. So long as the fundamental necessity of praxis is not conceded, there is little hope for appreciation of the thinking which liberation theology tries to engender.'[9]

It has taken about 2,000 years for the Christian church to realize that the triune God is not only to be adored and worshipped, but also to be emulated and followed. 'Be ye therefore perfect as your heavenly Father is perfect' is a commandment that can be taken seriously if we have a theology of a classless society. How can we follow the co-equality of Father, Son and Holy Spirit in a society which is based on capitalism and class structures? The quest of our age is for socialism, classlessness, egalitarianism, equality of opportunity, equality in spite of all distinctions, and a world brotherhood in the model of the Holy Trinity. A dialectic influence of worship and life, teaching and practice is possible only in a classless society based on this model.

The Quest of Sexism and Racism

The quest for a trinitarian theology, ethics, life-style and praxis is also discernible in the present women's lib or the liberation movement of the women of the whole world. It is a pity that theologians of the World Council of Churches are also ready to equate sexism with racism. The distinction between man and woman is in the order of creation though that distinction in essence is no reasonable basis for the lack of equality between the sexes. Functional equality is not meant for man and woman, though the same is meant for people of different races. A trinitarian theology of equality in spite of distinction is most applicable in the case of man and woman. Pauline reference to the equality of Jew and Greek, slave and free, male and female in the body of Christ in Galatians 3:28 does not exclude the functional distinction that man and woman have in the historical order. It is after the resurrection that there is no giving and receiving in marriage but all are like angels. What is significant is that the different functions of the father and mother in a family do not make one superior and the other inferior. The classic phrase, 'distinct but equal' is applicable at a deeper level between man and woman than between the races.

A trinitarian theology of a classless society will shed a bright light on the existing theology of fanatic and over-enthusiastic women who want to re-edit the Bible changing the prayer our Lord taught to 'Our Mother who art in heaven', and also on the male-dominated society which is not ready to accept women as equal. In the above-mentioned article, Frederick Herzog quotes from a book edited by Glenn R. Bucher,[10]

18

which says that 'the Bible will have to be re-edited. Passages that reinforce the oppression of women and the gays (homosexuals) must be revised, re-interpreted, or eliminated altogether.' How silly are such demands! If God is addressed 'Our Mother who art in heaven' we will replace male superiority with female superiority. If the chairman is addressed as chairperson or moderator, no one knows whether it is a man or a woman presiding. If there is no biological distinction between man and woman, gays have a point to defend their more dubious activities. The only solution for such insoluble problems of women's liberation movements and the like is to accept the trinitarian theology of a classless society, distinction and equality at the same breath without nullifying either. Although none of the apostles was a woman there is no inferiority for women in the Orthodox ecclesiology. The Blessed Virgin Mary as mother of God has a superior place in the church to the twelve apostles.

The application of the trinitarian theology 'one substance and three persons' is capable of asserting an essential equality in spite of functional distinctions not only between man and woman, but also between employer and employee, seller and purchaser, teacher and taught, ruler and ruled, priesthood and laity, and manager and labourer. Does not an officer in the Indian Administrative Service respect his elder brother who is a farmer? Do they not eat round the same table? Would a Chief Minister or Prime Minister say that he or she is superior to his or her mother or father, who may be illiterate? The equality of the personality of each in the Trinity is due to the sameness of the *ousia* or essence of Godhead. Similarly, all human beings are equal owing to the sameness of the image of God in all human beings. There is a great need for a theology of a classless society, taking the Trinity of Godhead as the model. After all, there is no absolute distinction in the Godhead over-ruling the unity and the solidarity.

The Quest of the Ecumenical Movements

The Faith and Order Commission is the theological pillar of the World Council of Churches. It has started many valuable

19

studies such as 'Giving Account of the Hope that is in us', 'The Unity of the Church and the Unity of Mankind,' and 'The Community of Women and Men in the Church'. But the 50th anniversary of the founding of the Faith and Order Commission (in Lausanne, Switzerland, 26–29th March 1977) is described by Lukes Vischer, the moving spirit and theologian behind it, in an Ecumenical Press Service bulletin as 'a demonstration against ecumenical half-heartedness'. The address by Philip Potter, the General Secretary was entitled, 'The Unity of the Church: What is to be done?' Among the many things to be done is a new study on a theology of a classless society without being afraid of the communistic overtone of the title. The strength of Marxism is that Marx has borrowed the idea from his Judeo-Christian heritage and has made it a central rallying point attracting millions of the downtrodden towards it. Why should the ecumenical movement be afraid of the title of the study just because Marx has used the phrase classless society in relation to class war and as a means of attack on the bourgeois class?

The half-heartedness of the ecumenical movement is partly due to the fear of the western churches even for dialogue with other religions and ideologies, as manifested in the Nairobi Assembly when the report on it came to the plenary session for discussion and approval. The first report had to be sent back for re-drafting and it was mutilated to accommodate the so-called evangelicals who feared that dialogue would lead to syncretism. Is Jesus Christ so weak that we have to defend him from being absorbed by other religions as just one of the prophets? Does he not have a uniqueness of his own which will ultimately triumph by virtue of its own strength? Did the writer of the fourth gospel weaken the incarnation by using Philo's theory of the logos and carrying it further than Alexandrian Judaism and Greek neo-Platonism? Did the church Fathers like St. Basil the Great weaken the doctrine of Trinity by using terms such as *ousia* and *hypostasis* prevalent in the non-Christian religions and ideologies of his day? Are we not courageous enough to believe that Jesus Christ is the way, the truth and the life for all humanity and all religions and ideologies and that truth will ultimately triumph owing to its intrinsic value? Is his place at the centre of secular history between BC and AD accidental, or given by others out of charity or one which he earned in his own right? If the doctrine of trinity is the one and only revelation of God, why should we be afraid of dialogue with monism, dualism, tritheism, exclusive monotheism or even atheism?

The whole world is looking up towards the W.C.C. and all other ecumenical concerns for a courageous stand for the church and the whole of humanity with Jesus Christ as the one absolute revelation, and the Holy Trinity as the only true doctrine of God for all religions and ideologies. Any theology that is true must be the theology for all people. There is no absoluteness in any part-existence. Christ is for all and all are for Christ and his theology is one of a classless society, 'putting down the mighty from their thrones and exalting those of low degree.' The ecumenical movement must work for the unity of the church and the unity of mankind.

The Quest for a World Government and Peace with Justice

Historians of the calibre of Arnold J. Toynbee have expressed the quest of humanity for a world government. It is doubtful whether the rich countries of the world will ever agree to the idea. However it is gratifying that Jimmy Carter in the address already referred to said, 'I believe that the developing countries must acquire fuller participation in the global economic decision-making process. Some progress has been made in this regard by the expanding participation of developing countries in the International Monetary Fund.'[11] But this nominal participation in the I.M.F. or World Bank is not going to elevate the status of the poor to such a degree that it will create an egalitarian society in the whole world. The west will have to study afresh the self-emptying (kenotic) Christology and see the essence of Christian love, not in a hand-out but in a self-emptying self-giving. The rich in the east will also have to do the same. The inadequacies of Christian theology in the past were its substitutionary theory of atonement, its doctrine of cheap grace, its exclusive ecclesiology and its denominationalism. Hence there is the further need to study

21

the cosmic Christology in Colossians 1:15-20 and other New Testament passages. The need of a world government is part of a Christian theology of a classless society as there can be no democratic government of the future which would not carry the people with it. Christian theology is not the prerogative of a few intellectuals, but the faith of the whole people of God.

There is hardly any document of a serious nature which deals with world government or international economic order which does not speak of peace with justice. The American President himself is of the opinion that 'The search for peace and justice mean also respect for human dignity. The United Nations is the global forum dedicated to the peace and well-being of every individual, no matter how weak or how poor. But we have allowed its human rights machinery to be ignored and sometimes politicized. There is much that can be done to strengthen it.'[12]

Peace with justice means social justice and not mere personal justice meted out to an offended individual. Lately, some evangelicals like Dr. Ronald J. Sider, the young American chairman of Evangelicals for Social Action, have begun to recognize this. In an article in *International Review of Mission,* he describes five conflicting viewpoints:

1. Evangelism is the primary mission of the church.
2. Evangelism is *one* basic mission of the church.
3. The primary mission of the church is the corporate body of believers.
4. The conversion of individuals and the political restructuring of society are equally important parts of salvation.
5. Evangelism is politics because salvation is social justice.

He defends a 6th viewpoint that evangelism and social justice are distinct, but equal. To quote:

> Only if we biblical Christians throw ourselves into the struggle for social justice for the wretched of the earth so unequivocally that the poor and the oppressed know beyond all question that we will risk all in the struggle against economic and political oppression—only then will Third World theologians be willing to hear our critique of unbiblical definitions of salvation. And only then will the oppressed of the earth be able to hear our good news about the risen Lord.[13]

The Quest for a Christian Communism

McCarthysm of the 1950's is dead and yet it is still very much alive in many parts of the world. I am afraid there will be many of my good Christian friends who will brand me a communist after reading this book; but I am not a revolutionary like Camilo Torres, the Colombian Roman Catholic priest who was not only laicized in 1965 by the hierarch, but also killed in ambush by a military patrol, because he had preached violence and joined the Army of National Liberation. In his writings there is a section dealing with communism in the church. First, he points out the unscientific and indefensible attitude of many towards communism. He says:

> To discredit a bridge it suffices to call it rotten. To make people persecute a dog, although it may be a noble one, it is enough to use the adjective rabid. In the early Christian era, to call an individual Christian was a way to outlaw him. Later the enemy of the Roman Empire was called barbarian to justify persecuting him. Before the French Revolution free thinkers, liberals, democrats, plebians, were persecuted. At present the best way to unleash persecution against a person regarded as a threat to the ruling class is by calling him communist. [14]

He also adds that the perspective which views communism as the principal evil is 'not very theological and not very scientific'.

Camilo then goes on to the positive suggestion that Christianity should be pro-humanity instead of being anti-anything. To quote:

> If this good of all mankind cannot be achieved except by changing the temporal structures, it would be sinful for a Christian to oppose change. Only the discriminating and scientific criticism of communism with the well-being of all men in mind justified not an anti-communist but a scientific attitude that implies rejecting everything anti-scientific. [15]

The three suggestions he had to propose to the Colombian clergy are valid for all clergy and all Christians of all countries. They are:

1. More concern should be shown for the well-being of mankind than for the protection of mankind from communism.

2. The clergy should discontinue occasional and paternalistic charity as a habitual form of action.
3. The members of clergy should concentrate their efforts on preparing members of the laity to transform the temporal structures from the ground up and thus attack the origin of social problems.

To the question 'Should communism be outlawed?' his answer is:

> From the theoretical point of view, I believe that the best weapons to combat ideas are ideas, the best way to combat political movements is by showing greater efficiency in the use of power. Therefore the laws against political ideas or movements are, in my opinion, a demonstration of weakness.
> However, in any country where communists are actually excluded from public office, from the right to be elected, from occupying chairs at the university, and in many cases from the right to study and work, it would be less hypocritical to outlaw them officially.[16]

How wise and Christian are the above quotations from the revolutionary Christian priest! In my opinion, he is arguing a more sympathetic attitude towards communism by the Christian church. To this writer it seems that atheistic communism is a reaction to the class structured church which does not manifest human brotherhood under the Fatherhood of God. Therefore, a theology of a classless society, if implemented, can defeat atheistic communism as well as dialectic materialism. Atheistic communism is only a passing stage towards a theistic classless society which accepts God as the owner of all the wealth and God's children all over the world are treated as right inheritors of God's wealth. The basis of this classless society is not Marxism but the eternal love of the Holy Trinity in eternal action which nullifies inequalities and creates an essential equality without discarding distinctions. Christian revelation is the basis of such a classless society.

The Quest for a Theology Come of Age

Dietrich Bonhoeffer's view that man has come of age does not make Christian theology irrelevant, if it is the right type of

24

theology or theology come of age. Rudolph Bultmann's demythology is not sufficient for a relevant theology for our times. Leslie Dewart's view deserves special attention. He says, 'the integration of theism with today's everyday experience requires not merely the demythologizing of Scripture but the more comprehensive dehellenizing of dogma, and specially that of the Christian doctrine of God.'[17]

The thesis of this book is that only the Christian doctrine of Trinity is the theology come of age and that it has a decisive role to play in every day experience. A theology come of age must have the following characteristics:

1. It should not support pyramidical hierarchy, autocracy or bourgeois life style, but must stand for collegiality, democracy and proleterian life style.

2. The hermeneutics of the church should not be on the basis of *sola scriptura,* nor on the individualistic interpretation of the Scriptures, but based on sound Christian theology which has withstood the tempest of the past and will be oriented towards the future. We should not be apologetic of true dogma, but allow the revealed dogma to speak to our times through the Scriptures and through the experience of the church universal.

3. Christology has to be reinterpreted not only for the church but also for other religions and ideologies, presenting Christ as the only given divine-human pneumatic centre of the church and the world at large. Oscar Cullmann's *Christ and Time* has a special relevance here. Christ as logos is still at work inside and outside the church and he is present in part wherever man thinks logically, reasonably, even in rationalism. There is no goodness anywhere apart from God and Christ being God is present in goodness everywhere. His incarnation, however, is the only dependable criterion of the good. He is the yardstick to measure all yardsticks all over the world. Christ belongs to the church and the world.

4. We need an ecclesiology which includes the visible and the latent or hidden church. Camilo Torres has said, 'From the strictly theoretical point of view, when one speaks of the church, one speaks of all the baptized, both those baptized by sacrament and those consecrated by intention.'[18] The

whole of humanity is the potential church and needs the loving concern of the baptized community without any discrimination against the unbaptized.

5. Theology come of age will not be over enthusiastic on the growth of church membership as the sole intention of Christian mission. We need a new theory of mission which takes the need of man as the motivation for mission, the last commission and the greatest commandments as two sides of the same coin.

6. Christian theology of tomorrow should take the transcendence and immanence of God as equally valid, history and eternity as equally important, individual and society as inseparable, the person and the family as a unity, the nation and the world as one nuclear family and above all the Holy Trinity as the one key that unlocks all locks.

7. The Fatherhood of God and the brotherhood of humanity must be practised, irrespective of the sin of disunity as 'with God all things are possible'.

8. Our eschatology also has to be both this worldly and otherworldly taking realized and apocalyptic eschatologies as of equal significance.

2
SIN AND CLASS FORMATION

'So God created man in his own image, in the image of God he created *him*; male and female he created *them*' (Gen. 1:27). God created a nuclear family in his own image because God himself is a nuclear family.

The most ancient institution in history is the family. Animal families are instinctive and temporary, human families are spiritual and life-long and God the triune family is divine and eternal. The life-long bond of the family is asserted in the Markan version of our Lord's discourse on the indissolubility of marriage. 'From the beginning of creation God made them male and female. For this reason a man shall leave his father and mother and be joined to his wife, and the two shall become one. So they are no longer two but one. What therefore God has joined together, let not man put asunder.' (Mark 10: 6-9.) The child is the manifestation of the truth of the statement of our Lord that they are one body.

'A family divided against itself cannot stand.' God is a family which is never divided against itself and stands eternally as one. Fatherhood, sonship and motherhood are in the one Godhead without beginning and end. He is eternal Father (Isa. 6: 9) because he has the eternal Son in himself. He did not become a Father in time, for he is the same yesterday, to-day and for ever. The Holy Spirit is pictured as mother in Christian art and sculpture for God has never been without the love dimension, predominant in the mother more than in the father. 'As one whom his mother comforts, so I will comfort you' (Isa. 66.13)[19].

An ideal family, like the Blessed Trinity, is a unity in trinity and a trinity in unity though it is never fully manifested so in our fallen order. There is neither selfishness nor jealousy in any member of a perfect home as all live for others and all

27

resources are shared for the common benefit and the benefit of each one. In Christian theology, God is not a monad and so his plan about man is 'It is not good that man should be alone' (Gen. 2: 18). Hence St. Athanasius and St. Basil made rules for solitary monks to live in communities. Monastic communities ought to be ideal spiritual nuclear families in which the role of the superior should not be that of an authoritarian monarch, but that of the father of a family.

It is significant that in the second, chronologically earlier creation story (Gen. 2: 4–25), Adam could not find a life-partner in any of the subhuman species which he named and that Eve was made out of his own bones, so that he shouted in ecstatic joy at the first sight of her, 'This at last is bone of my bones and flesh of my flesh; she shall be called woman, because she was taken out of man' (Gen. 2: 23). My thesis that God is a nuclear family and that humanity must ultimately become a nuclear family in the ultimate kingdom of God in the model of the Holy Trinity, needs elaboration which is not possible in this small book.

The Holy Trinity is not merely functional as Hans Küng depicts. 'The trinitarian formulas aim not at an "immanent" but an "economic" theology of the Trinity, not at an inner divine three-oneness by itself but a oneness in the history of salvation (economic) of Father, Son and Spirit in the encounter with us, not about God in himself but God for us, how through Jesus he himself acted for us in the Spirit, the action on which the reality of our salvation depends.'[20] The Fathers of the Church spent a great deal of time showing that God in his essence is triune. The keystone of Christian faith about God that distinguishes it from faith in Allah of Islam, *Nirguna Brahma* (Attributions Absolute) of Sankara and polytheism of popular Hinduism and every other theology of the world, is that God is eternally, ontologically and functionally Trinity. The unknowable and inscrutable God has revealed himself as Father, Son and Holy Spirit, one God, love in eternal action, co-equal and of one essence. There is no truth greater than the ultimate truth that God is eternally Trinity.

Sin Ushers in Divisions

Edwin Lewis of Drew University, in his book *The Creator and the Adversary,* takes the stand that the adversary is uncreated but active only after creation and inactive after the consummation when the adversary will be bound. The role of the adversary is discreative and destructive and never creative and constructive. The traditional teaching of the church is that satan is a fallen angel. The view that evil is the absence of good will not stand in the light of biblical teaching. Evil is a positive reality that crept into the realm of light in the form of a serpent. The fall of Eve was when she was alone. When her fellowship with God and Adam changed into complicity with satan, sin crept into her life and through her to her husband's life. Satan does not come to any of us as undisguised satan. Cosmic evil appears in the guise of too much profit or extreme poverty, extraordinary beauty or intolerable ugliness, lust for power or belittling despair, the vanity of the present evil world or doubt about the future, selfish instinct or sexual passion.

'Now the serpent was more subtle than any other creature that the Lord God had made.' All temptations are subtle desires, cunning thoughts. Satan asks, 'Did God say . . . ?' Then he says the opposite of what God said. God had said, 'in the day that you eat of it you shall die'; and satan said, 'You will not die' (Gen. 3:4). 'So when the woman saw that the tree was good for food, and that it was delight to the eyes, and that the tree was to be desired to make one wise, she took of its fruit . . . and ate; . . . and she gave some to her husband . . . and he ate,' is the summary of what happened in many days in the life of the one who gradually yielded to the temptation and fell.

The story of the fall is not to be used as a cloak for male superiority. The fall was a corporate event. 'Then the eyes of both were opened, and they knew that they were naked; and they sewed fig leaves together and made themselves aprons' (3:7). Though Eve first plucked the fruit, she was slowly tempted to it, but Adam ate the fruit without any hesitation. When God appeared in the garden as usual, both had hidden themselves, but it was Adam who was questioned first. His answer was an indirect attack on God himself, 'The woman

29

whom *thou gavest* to be with me, she gave me fruit of the tree and I ate'. Eve was no better for she also refused to accept the guilt but threw it on the serpent. When the Lord knew their futile efforts to hide their own nakedness by the drying fig-leaves, he was gracious to both, 'And the Lord God made for Adam and for his wife garments of skins, and clothed them' (3:20). The result of the fall was not only in the sense of shame but also in the lost solidarity of the family. Cain killed his own brother. The murder of brother by brother was due to the hatred of the mother by the father, the wife by the husband. Adam, who regarded Eve as flesh of his own flesh before the fall, has started to blame her for his own fall also. Class hatred started not with Cain, but with Adam's fall. When the Lord questioned Adam, he had already isolated himself from his wife and posed an attitude of self-justification.

Sin is always the harbinger of divisions. Sin is the sense of being rejected by God which expresses itself by hating one's own brother. The sinner is afraid that he or she will be killed by the other and has a deep sense of insecurity. This is also because security is only in unity with God and fellowmen. The courage to be (Paul Tillich) is possible only in harmony with God and our fellowmen. The world we live in is fear-stricken. There is a criminal waste of God-given resources for an armament race of unprecedented destructive potentialities owing to the insecurity of nations in a class-ridden society. Capitalists consider communists to be atheistic devils and communists consider capitalists to be enemies of progress. The former needs a humanism of universal brotherhood and the latter a theology of God's Fatherhood if the class war is to be avoided. The means of effecting such a reconciliation is not the perpetuation of hatred, but a repentance for our own sin and a readiness to enter into frank and sincere dialogue between the classes.

The contemporary situation is far from that of Cain the sinner killing Abel the righteous (1 John 3:11–18). We have 2 Cains in every situation, in every country and in the international scene. Both have stopped taking God into the decisive role he deserves. Like the parable of the two sons who were asked by the father to go and work in the vineyard (Matt.

21:28–32), neither obeyed in theory and in practice. There is individualistic piety among the capitalists with a purely vertical religion and no desire for a classless society, and there is a secular religion of communism with no vertical devotion to God, a humanistic religion which is quite inadequate for a man who is created in the image of God. Both the groups are in the forefront of the armaments race. The suicidal situation will continue as long as the class distinction and class suspicion and hatred continue. It is foolish to ask the United States to throw away the destructive bombs unilaterally as Bertrand Russell suggested. All the efforts of both the parties must be concentrated on implementing the brotherhood of man under the Fatherhood of God. As St. John asks, 'If any one has the world's goods and sees his brother in need, yet closes his heart against him, how does God's love abide in him?' Again, 'If anyone says, "I love God" and hates his brother, he is a liar for he who does not love his brother whom he has seen, cannot love God whom he has not seen. And this commandment we have from him, that he who loves God should love his brother also' (1 John 4:20f).

It is now more or less agreed by thinkers round the world that we cannot have infinite progress in a finite world in the realm of finite goods. The economic disparity between the rich and the poor is the clearest manifestation of class distinctions. Dignity of the person is now the birth-right only of the rich even in countries where democracy is practised. All the present talk about human rights will be meaningful only when all share the rights in all the countries. This cannot happen as long as class war exists. A simpler life style must be practised by all people to effect the unity of all.

The Saga of Cain and Abel

Sin and the formation of classes cannot be explained in better terms than by allusion to the story of Cain and Abel. Adam and Eve could have been kept in the garden of Eden if they had confessed their sins and not thrown the blame on each other. The psychology of a class society started with the coming of sin. 'I will put enmity between you and the woman, and

31

between your seed and her seed; I will greatly multiply your pain in childbearing, and in pain you shall bring forth children . . . Cursed is the ground because of you; in toil you shall eat of it' (Gen. 3:16, 17). Sin brings enmity and class war because humanity has become a hotch-potch of satanic seed and human seed. Pleasant labour has become painful toil for the human lot. The multiplication of the pain of childbearing is not only in the pain of delivery, which is being eased by medical science, but in the sorrow of parents for having begotten such disobedient children. When the people are wicked, nature is also vile, full of thorns and thistles. The fall of Adam was also the fall of nature. The exploitation of energy, forests, natural resources and all the minerals of the world by the selfish, competitive, accumulative western society is not the sin of the west alone, but the sin of man everywhere. The difference is only in degree. There is a vestige of religion even in the fallen man. When Adam knew Eve and she conceived and bore a son, Cain, he said, 'I have gotten a man with the help of the Lord' (Gen. 4:1). But when Abel, the second son is born, this sentence is not found on the lips of Adam, because he is gradually losing his religion as so often happens in our fallen world.

'Now Abel was a keeper of sheep, and Cain a tiller of the ground.' Is there a class distinction here? Not necessarily. The mental alienation of Cain from Abel took place when he found that the Lord had rejected his offering. The most important lesson of the story of Abel and Cain is that all the horizontal alienations between man and man are the end result of the separation from God. One who thinks he is rejected by God cannot receive his own brother as brother, but would rather kill him by any treachery conceivable. The innocent Abels of history are always victimized by the jealous Cains.

Though Cain brought an offering to God before his brother, no special word of appreciation is mentioned about it by the writer of Genesis. But about Abel's offering it is written, 'Abel brought of the firstlings of his flock and of their fat portions . . . Cain was very angry and his countenance fell.' With whom was he angry? He was angry with God and his brother at the same time, but as he could not kill God, he killed his own brother. There is no partiality in the act of God. Cain is told that his offerings were rejected because he did not do well. 'If you do well, will you not be accepted?' Why did God reject Cain's offering? In the course of time he must have brought an offering to the Lord, perhaps when there had been some failure of rain or sun, and the intention must have been selfish. Did he bring his first-fruits as Abel did? Was he in the habit of giving his best to the Lord every year? Cain is our modern man who worships the Lord to get some favour from him, and when he does not get his prayers answered he becomes jealous of those whose prayers are answered. Sin is crouching at the door of everyone who harbours hatred for his brother. When God gave a warning to Cain, 'You must master it', Cain should have gone to Abel and apologized to him for being jealous of him in his own heart. Instead, he beguiled Abel to his own field and while both of them were there, 'Cain rose up against his brother Abel and killed him'. The downward trend between brother and brother has reached the murder-level of enmity passing though the class formation.

The perennial question from God to the oppressing brother whether he is the employer or the employee, the master or the servant, the white or the black, the have's or the have-not's, the rulers or the ruled, the elder or the younger, is 'where is Abel your brother?' In a classless society the answer would be, 'We are sharing everything as in a nuclear family and the brother and myself are here together around one dining table of the dining hall and above all, around the eucharistic table of the common eldest brother of us all, our Lord Jesus Christ.' In a class-ridden society, on the other hand, the answer is, 'I do not know; am I my brother's keeper?' Capitalism will survive in the world only if the labourers also become owners and shareholders and then it will hardly be capitalism as we understand it to-day.

The policy of apartheid is the same old answer of Cain, 'Am I my brother's keeper?' Yes, every elder brother is the keeper of the younger brother, and yet he does not call himself the keeper, but the brother. Similarly every younger brother must be grateful to the elder brothers and work with and for the whole family, regarding the family as the unit to which both the elder and the younger belong gladly and proudly.

In a society where one class exploits another or brother kills brother by word or deed or attitude, the eternal and loving Father asks a threatening question, 'What have you done? The voice of your brother's blood is crying to me from the ground . . . You shall be a fugitive and a wanderer on the earth.' This is written in the stuff of nature. The earth is created for one family and not for many families which war with each other. 'The meek shall inherit the earth', our Lord said in the Sermon on the Mount, the ethics of the kingdom of God or the nuclear family of God. The oppressors of history are the fugitives of history in the long run. Arnold J. Toybnee's painstaking and exhaustive *A Study of History* has proved it beyond doubt. Cains do not inherit the earth, they wander from place to place afraid of the nemesis they expect at any moment. The pathetic cry of Cain to the Lord is, 'My punishment is greater than I can bear; Behold thou has driven me this day away from the ground; and from thy face I shall be hidden; and I shall be a fugitive and a wanderer on the earth, and whoever finds me will slay me.' The October Revolution of 1917 and almost all revolutions we know of are the overthrow of the oppressing class by the oppressed in the providence of God according to the wrath and love of God in one act.

Strangely enough, the vengeance of God is not limited to Cains who kill the innocent brothers, but falls also on those who slay the oppressing Cains. That is why the merciful Lord told Cain, 'Not so! If any one slays Cain, vengeance shall be taken on him sevenfold. And the Lord put a mark on Cain, lest any who came upon him should kill him.' The fear of revenge is increasing with each succeeding generation. Hence Lamech of the sixth generation from Cain,who killed a young man for striking him,bemoans to his two wives, 'If Cain is avenged sevenfold, truly Lamech seventy-sevenfold' (4:24). The whole episode of Cain is to teach us that a house divided against itself cannot stand. Humanity has only two alternatives to choose from, either to move towards a classless society of a nuclear family or to perish by perpetuating the class structure of our world divided between the rich and the poor, the Brahmins and the Harijans, the whites and the coloured, the capitalists and the communists, the man and the woman, the father and his alienated son and so on. The alternative can

34

also be seen as one between a quick evolution to a classless society controlled by a world government or a bloody revolution of mutual annihilation. A third way is not clear even on our horizon.

Babel of Sin and Pentecost of Salvation

Babel which scatters the various classes of humanity with Pentecost which gathers the many into one. 'Now the whole earth had one language and few words.' A second beginning after the deluge is also in the nuclear family of Noah extended to include the whole earth. The many classes created by the murder of Cain are destroyed by the flood,keeping a remnant of a classless society to continue the human race. The ark of Noah, which the fathers of the church following 1 Peter 3:20f. have compared to the church, was one family in perfect harmony with 'all the beasts and all the cattle that were with him in the ark' (Gen. 8:1). But the descendants of Noah repeat the mistake of Adam and Eve in a new manner. Their motto is not to adore the name of the all adorable God who saved them through an ark, but to make themselves into a class with a name for themselves. The serpent is not mentioned here but they had the serpent in their hearts to tempt them. Their desire was to have one human class of people who would be able to dethrone God and enthrone themselves in his place. Their determination to fight against God is expressed in the classic sentence, 'Come, let us build ourselves a city, and a tower with its top in the heavens, and let us make a name for ourselves, lest we be scattered abroad upon the face of the earth'. They wanted a classless society in the safe security of the plain in the land of Shinar without the protecting hand of God and without the responsibility and suffering of scattered life. It is impossible to have a classless society in its perfection if it is without God as the centre, and without the whole earth as its earthly limits. The mistake of the Babel community was that they wanted to put themselves in the centre. Hence, it is parochial, limited, self-defeating and bound to fail.

God punishes before he saves as justice demands punishment of the guilty. 'And the Lord came down to see the city and the tower, which the sons of men had built.' He destroyed the man-centred humanism to pave the way for the theo-centric humanism at Pentecost. As it always happens they made themselves their destiny and lost their destiny. If they had gone down to the valleys to bury those who had been drowned in the flood and to cultivate the fertile land, they would have found their lives by losing themselves in the service of others. Their ambition to go up ended in their punishment to go down the ladder of life. Their desire to communicate only between themselves without communicat-ing to God ended in the loss of communication and in the Babel of tongues. 'They left off building the city.'

The world is full of incomplete towers of Babel. They repeat to us the same old story that only that which God builds will be complete and perfect. The kingdom of God is the city of God whose 'builder and maker is God'. 'Apart from me, you can do nothing', says our God. Pride created a class of exclusiveness in Babel and God scattered it. The classless society that God wants to build is that which includes the whole of humanity into one class of human brotherhood, irrespective of all cultural, linguistic, racial and ethnic distinc-tions. This was what he did at Pentecost.

The importance of Pentecost can never be overestimated in a study of a theology of a classless society. Pentecost was the antidote to Babel. 'When the day of Pentecost had come, they were *all together* in one place.' 'They were filled with the Holy Spirit and began to speak in other tongues.' The tragedy of Babel was that every one spoke a language that no one else understood and the remedy was that every one could speak in the tongue of others. 'We hear them telling in our own tongues the mighty works of God.' The problem of our class-structure society is that the employer cannot speak in the tongue of the employees and vice versa. No one is interested in the mighty works of God, but only in the mighty works of their own selves. The moneyed class are primarily interested in erecting high towers for themselves and their own children and not in building comfortable houses for their employees. Eighteen classes of people are mentioned in Acts 2:9–11, but they could all understand the language of the Galileans. They were fused into one class by the working of the Holy Spirit and amazingly they shared everything in common, of which more will be said later. A comparison of Babel and Pentecost points out a number of contrasts:

Babel	Pentecost
1. Scattering of one class to many.	Gathering of many classes into one.
2. Confusion of languages 'that they may not understand one another's speech'.	The miracle of the language of love that all could understand.
3. Man's futile effort to become God ends in the loss of humanity.	God's gracious descent to humanity creates a divine community.
4. The unfinished, forsaken city of man. 'Let us build ourselves a city.'	The growing city of God on earth. 'In Jerusalem . . . devout men from every nation under heaven.'
5. Pride goes before a fall. 'Let us make a name for ourselves.'	'Whoever calls the name of the Lord shall be saved.'
6. Punishment for all atheistic efforts.	Reward for the theistic community.
7. The destiny of the unredeemed first Adam.	'The destiny of the redeemed children of the second Adam.'
8. There is no repentance for the doomed.	'Repent and be baptized, every one of you in the name of Jesus Christ for the forgiveness of your sins.'
9. The crooked generation of Noah ends up in many classes, fighting with each other.	'Save yourselves from this crooked generation.'
10. Flight from the presence of God.	'There were added that day about three thousand souls.'

11. The failure of materialism. 'Come, let us make bricks and burn them thoroughly.'	The success of a divine humanism. 'The promise is to . . . all that are far off.'
12. From Shinar to the ends of the earth.	In Jerusalem from the ends of the earth, 'they devoted themselves to the apostles' teaching and fellowship, to the breaking of bread and prayers'.

'Come, Holy Spirit come, fuse us together into a classless society.'

3
PRACTISE SOCIAL JUSTICE OR PERISH

What the Bible Teaches on Social Justice

There are innumerable passages in Scripture on social justice, but the church has very conveniently ignored them. Of all the prophets of the Old Testament, Amos, the first of the literary prophets, was the most outspoken about it since he could not tolerate the accumulation of wealth in the hands of a few in the days of Jeroboam II in Israel and Uzziah in Judah. His cry for justice sounded 2700 years ago still remains a cry in the wilderness. The opening sentence, 'The Lord roars from Zion, and utters his voice from Jerusalem' may be repeated replacing Zion with New York, or Jerusalem with Rome or Calcutta. His charges then are as relevant to-day as in the 8th century BC. Notice some of his observations on the lack of justice and prevalent exploitations that existed before the fall of Samaria in 722 BC.

a. 'They did not remember the covenant of brotherhood' (1:9). There would be no exploitation today if we remembered the covenant of human brotherhood which would in turn hasten the unity of the church with the unity of mankind.

b. 'He pursued his brother with the sword, and cast off all pity' (1:11). Man is now able to annihilate his brethren with bombs, with little or no pity whatsoever.

c. 'I will not revoke the punishment because they have ripped up women with child in Gilead, that they might enlarge their border' (1:13). The play *Muntu* performed at the fifth Assembly of the W.C.C. at Nairobi had a climactic sentence: 'When the missionaries came, we had the land and they had the Bible; now we have the Bible and they have our land'. This is an exaggerated picture of the connection between western mission and colonialism, from which the developing countries are liberating themselves—Ian Smith, not withstanding! South Africa will also be liberated without much delay.

d. 'They sell the righteous for silver and the needy for a pair of shoes—they that trample the head of the poor into the dust of the earth and turn aside the way of the afflicted' (2:6,7). Bonded labour is still not wiped out in India.

e. 'You made the Nazarites drink wine' (2:12). 'Hear this word, you cows of Bashan, who are in the mountain of Samaria, who oppress the poor, who crush the needy, who say to their husbands, "Bring, that we may drink!" ' (4:1). According to *Time* magazine dated 16th May 1977 United States revenues from the rackets are staggering: gross income 48 billion dollars and net income 25.3 billion dollars. Alcoholism is an increasing menace in our modern world.

f. 'I will smite the winter house with the summer house; and the houses of ivory shall perish and great houses shall come to an end' (3:15, 6:4). This took place literally in the Soviet Union 1917. Still, palatial private houses are on the increase in the countries of free enterprise and mixed economy, leaving the teeming millions in slums, miserable huts and on the pavements! The punishment of God will overtake us also if we do not curtail our personal luxuries to build houses for the homeless and to provide jobs for the increasing number of jobless people on our small earth.

g. 'You turn justice to wormwood and cast down righteousness to the earth' (5:7). 'You who afflict the righteous, who take a bribe, and turn aside the needy in the gate . . . Seek good, and not evil, that you may live . . . establish justice in the gate' (5:12–15). Amos would have thundered louder had he lived today and known the exploitation of the poor countries by the multi-national corporations. Small bribery of Amos' days has now grown to the magnitude of Lockheed scandals and the like.

h. 'I hate, I despise your feasts, and I take no delight in your solemn assemblies . . . Take away from me the noise of your songs; to the melody of your harps I will not listen. But let justice roll down like waters, and righteousness like an ever-flowing stream' (5:21–24). The present counterparts of this injustice are to be found in certain church festivals with a colossal waste of money and energy, and also in some modern weddings with their pomp and show of wealth.

i. 'Hear this, you who trample upon the needy, and bring the poor of the land to an end, saying, "When will the new moon be over . . . that we may make the ephah small and the shekel great, and deal deceitfully with false balances, that we may buy the poor for silver and the needy for a pair of sandals and sell the refuse of the wheat?" ' (8:4–6). Black-marketing, false balances and the like have now taken the form of unjust international trade practices in favour of the rich nations. Aid is extended to the poor nations to cover up the sins practised in trade.

Isaiah also has a number of things to say about the need for social justice. In the very first chapter he is the spokesman for God telling us: 'What to me is the multitude of your sacrifices? . . . Bring no more vain offerings; incense is an abomination to me . . . I will not listen . . . cease to do evil, learn to do good; seek justice, correct oppressions; defend the fatherless, plead for the widow.' Again in chapter 5 he adds. 'Woe to those who join house to house, who add field to field, until there is no more room . . . Surely many houses shall be desolate, large and beautiful houses, without inhabitant . . . Woe to those who call evil good and good evil, who put darkness for light and light for darkness . . . Woe to those who are heroes at drinking wine and valiant men in mixing strong drink, who acquit the guilty for a bribe, and deprive the innocent of his right.'

But a classless society will dawn with the messianic age according to Isaiah 11. 'The wolf shall dwell with the lamb, and the leopard shall lie down with the kid, and the calf and the lion and the fatling together, and a little child shall lead them. The cow and the bear shall feed, their young shall lie down together; and the lion shall eat straw like the ox . . . They shall not hurt or destroy in all my holy mountain; for the earth shall be full of the knowledge of the Lord as the waters cover the sea.' Even Tyre, after seventy years of punishment will practise social justice. 'Her merchandise and her hire will be dedicated to the Lord; it will not be stored or hoarded, but her merchandise will supply abundant food and fine clothing for those who dwell before the Lord' (Isa. 23:18).

The positive message of the old Testament Prophets on this topic is summarized in Micah 6:7–8: 'Will the Lord be pleased with thousands of rams, with ten thousands of rivers of oil? . . . He has showed you, O man, what is good; and what does the Lord require of you but to do justice, and to love kindness, and to walk humbly with your God?' (cf. Deut. 10:12f.). If we have justice, love and humility we will have a classless society in which all will be able to enjoy a dignified proletarian life-style. Our Lord's attack on the rich is found in Micah also: 'Your rich men are full of violence; your inhabitants speak lies, and their tongue is deceitful in their mouth. Therefore, I have begun to smite you' (6:12f). Micah must have thought of Solomon's sacrifice soon after the completion of the temple of Jerusalem, when he spoke against thousands of rams (cf.2 Chron.7:5). The need of the hour is a change from the life-style of Solomon to that of Jesus of Nazareth. Such a change is to be hastened not because of the energy crisis of which every one is talking, but because it is the will of God. *Time* magazine (16th May 1977) had a cartoon by Eddie Adams showing the burial ground of the big car with the tombstone inscription: 'Here lies our beloved big car, it ran out of gas'. Behind the energy crisis we must hear God's warning, 'I have begun to smite you' (Mic. 6:13). If we do not switch off the big car, we may be forced to switch on to the good old bicycle.

When we turn to the New Testament, the whole teaching of John the Baptist, Our Lord and St. James calls for special study. Only a few sample passages are quoted below:'And the multitudes asked him (John the Baptist) "What then shall we do?" And he answered them, "He who has two coats, let him share with him who has none; and he who has food, let him do likewise." Tax collectors also came to be baptized and said to him, "Teacher, what shall we do?" And he said to them, "Collect no more than is appointed you." Soldiers also asked him, "And we, what shall we do?" And he said to them, "Rob no one by violence or by false accusation, and *be content with your wages*." ' (Luke 3:10–14). In the classless society envisioned in this interpretation, every one will be content with his wages, including the contractor, the managing director, the general manager, and the wages will be more or less

42

egalitarian, on the basis of the work and need, and all work will be considered dignified.

The parable in Matthew 20 on equal wages for different amounts of work on the basis of need, and the parable in Matthew 25 where initiative to increase five talents to ten is specially rewarded on the basis of work, will be taken together to fix the wages of all. The one who buried the one talent is punished and all idle people will have to receive their due punishment gladly because they disobey the commandment, 'If anyone will not work, let him not eat' (2 Thess. 3: 10). The purpose of work will be the benefit of all and not the benefit of the worker alone. After all, what we need is a world family in which each member works for the whole family and the whole family takes care of the old and the sick who cannot work.

The ethics of the kingdom of God as taught in the Sermon on the Mount are certainly the ethics of a classless society. The earlier version of the beatitudes is in praise of material poverty on the part of the disciples and not just in praise of the hunger for spiritual things implied in 'Blessed are the poor in spirit'. The Lukan version reads, 'Blessed are you poor, for yours is the kingdom of God. Blessed are you that hunger now, for you shall be satisfied. Blessed are you that weep now, for you shall laugh. Blessed are you when men hate you . . . on account of the Son of man! Rejoice in that day and leap for joy, for behold, your reward is great in heaven; for so their fathers did to the prophets' (6: 20–23). There are 4 'Woe to you' passages soon after this addressed to those who are rich, full now, laugh now, and those of whom others speak well. In the classless society envisaged in Matthew 5-7, there is a common Father and no one is to be angry with his brother, or insult him. We are to make friends even with those who accuse us and draw us to the court. There is no question of following the Old Testament law of 'an eye for an eye' because enemies are to be treated as members of one's family. As God sends rain on the just and the unjust, we must give help to all people irrespective of their character, because doing good must be second nature of the citizens of the kingdom of God. We are not to judge our brothers and we are to be more concerned with the log in our own eye than with the speck in our brother's eye. The command not to give what is holy to the dogs has to do with mixing the sublime with the ridiculous and not with starving the dogs. God is not going to judge us on the basis of our prayers addressing him as 'Lord, Lord', but on the basis of our deeds in compliance with our servitude to the will of our Lord.

St. James, also one of the members of the Qumran Community which practised social justice, like John the Baptist, is very clear on the sinfulness of being rich in a poor world. He writes:

> My brethren show no partiality as you hold the faith of our Lord Jesus Christ, the Lord of glory. For if a man with gold rings and in fine clothing comes into your assembly, and a poor man in shabby clothing also comes in, and you pay attention to the one who wears the fine clothing and say, 'Have a seat here, please,' while you say to the poor man, 'Stand there,' or 'Sit at my feet,' have you not made distinctions among yourselves, and become judges with evil thoughts? Listen, my beloved brethren. Has not God chosen those who are poor in the world to be rich in faith and heirs of the kingdom which he has promised to those who love him? But you have dishonoured the poor man. Is it not the rich who oppress you, is it not they who drag you into court? . . . If you really fulfil the *royal law,* according to the Scripture, 'You shall love your neighbour as yourself,' you do well. But *if you show partiality, you commit sin,* and are convicted by the law as transgressor. (2: 1-9.)
>
> Come now, you rich, weep and howl for the miseries that are coming upon you. Your riches have rotted and your garments are moth-eaten . . . Behold, the wages of the labourers who mowed your fields, which you kept back by fraud, cry out; and the cries of the harvesters have reached the ears of the Lord of hosts. You have lived on the earth in luxury and in pleasure; you have fattened your hearts on a day of slaughter. You have condemned, you have killed the righteous man; he does not resist you. (5: 1–6.)

'Religion that is pure and undefiled', according to St. James, 'is to visit orphans and widows in their affliction, and to keep one-self unstained from the world' (1: 27). This has to be done, not as charity, but as the duty to one's own family.

St. Paul's background was different and so we do not see such a deep call for social justice in his letters. He was a rich Pharisee whose life was changed radically by the epoch-making Damascus experience of a personal encounter with the

Lord. He, the author of the hymn of love in 1 Corinthians 13 and the ethical chapters like Romans 12, Ephesians 5, Galatians 5, cannot be called to the defence of capitalism or free enterprise which ignores our brethren in need. His call, however, is for self-giving voluntary charity on the basis of the self-emptying of the incarnate God. We are asked to have the mind of Christ which would tell us to empty ourselves as he did (Phil. 2: 5-11), and his teaching on Christian giving in 2 Corinthians 8 and 9 would, if obeyed, create a classless society. 'I do not mean,' he writes, 'that others should be eased and you burdened, but that as a matter of equality your abundance at the present time should supply their want so that their abundance may supply your want, *that there may be equality*. As it is written, "He who gathered much had nothing over, and he who gathered little had no lack." ' (2 Cor. 8: 13–15). His kenotic christology of Philippians 2 is repeated here as a preamble in verse 9, 'For you know the grace of our Lord Jesus Christ, that though he was rich, yet for your sake he became poor, so that by his poverty you might become rich.' Is this not a call for a simpler living standard for the benefit of the poor in every country and in the developing countries in particular?

It seems to me that the time is now ripe for us to give as much importance to St. James and John the Baptist as we have given to St. Paul in the past. Martin Luther should not have described the epistle of James as the 'epistle of straw'. 'Justification by faith alone' is not the only canon in the New Testament to be used as a yardstick to study the whole Bible. The Holy Trinity must be the one canon used as the decisive doctrine with which to measure the Bible, theology and ethics.

When I say God is a nuclear family, I do not attribute the sexual limitation of creaturely families to God. When we say 'God is Father', we do not limit him to the male sex. We can also say 'God is Mother' without limiting him to the female sex. God's Fatherhood includes his Motherhood, Sonship and daughterhood as God is beyond sex and yet includes masculinity, femininity and essence. When Hinduism says that God is *Sat* (essence), *chit* (intelligence) and *anand* (bliss), it does not include personality. An impersonal God cannot be God the

45

Father, Mother, Son in one ontological essence and eternal functioning. The self-giving of God in Christ can be understood by us best in the context of the self-giving of the Father or the Mother or the Son for other members of the family. We are asked not only to adore and worship God, but also to be 'perfect as your heavenly Father is perfect'. There is no solution for the world's ills except a Trinitarian theology and ethics.

Who Kept the Torch Burning?

Worldliness which crept into the church with the bourgeois type of Christianity that emerged with Constantine and the Edict of Milan in 313 AD did not swallow the simplicity and essence of the church because of the monastic communities that emerged simultaneously as a protest against it. St. Antony sold everything he had and distributed it to the poor (285 AD), but later found the need to organize the various solitaries into a community and he did it in 305 AD. *Vita Antonii* (Life of Antony) by St. Athanasius gives us a clear picture of the beginning of monasticism in the church. The desert Fathers expressed their protest to this worldly life (from which comes the word asceticism) and strived to exercise self-control. (They could not have swallowed secular theology which puts all the emphasis on this present world and time and is allergic to other-worldly life.) The rules of Pachomius of Egypt and St. Basil the Great are marked by extreme austerity, prayer, fasting, manual labour, which made the proletarian life style enjoyable to the devotees of those days. The rules of St. Benedict (480-543) were a European adaptation of the rules of St. Basil. The Benedict orders of the Middle Ages 'practised and spread the ideal of voluntary poverty and produced many treatises on the ascetical life'.[21] The Christian churches the world over owe a debt of gratitude to the Franciscans, Dominicans, Benedictines and innumerable monastic orders in the church for having practised the self-emptying nature of Christian love and for keeping the torch of gospel ablaze in a world of feudalism and selfishness.

The Lutheran teaching on the total depravity of man, which

was also taught by John Calvin and others, and the emphasis on justification by faith alone led the protestant movement in general to be suspicious of monasticism. The corrupt life of the celibate priests and monks also helped in the decline of monasticism. But Protestantism should have found some other means of perpetuating the sharing fellowship of the early church in the reformation tradition as monasticism did in the eastern and western churches up to the present day. Individual freedom and the dignity of the person (Here I stand . . .) are in need of the corrective of social obligations and the dignity of the other person (Here we stand . . .) expressed in the solidarity of human existence. The often quoted passage of poet John Donne from his *Devotions* is worth quoting here also:

> No man is an island, entire of itself; every man is a piece of the continent, a part of the main; if a clod be washed away by the sea, Europe is the less, as well as if a promontory were, as well as if a man or of thy friends or of thine own were; any man's death diminishes me, because I am involved in mankind; and therefore never send to know for whom the bell tolls; it tolls for thee.[22]

I am not unaware of certain isolated Protestant communities like Taizé, but they are insufficient to manifest the classlessness of the Christian church.

Today, the torch-bearers of the theology of a classless society are not theologians, but scientists, economists, politicians, communists, socialists, the Club of Rome and participants in the 'Limits to Growth' discussions. Dr. C. T. Kurian, an Indian economist, quotes a western economist who said at a consultation in Geneva in 1973, 'We know better than ever, that the world is a whole; we are passengers in a space ship with finite resources'. Dr. Kurian commented:

> One of the most striking statements I have come across in following the 'Limits to Growth' discussion is the claim in a U.S. Senate Report that the American people consumed in the decade 1959-68 more of the resources of the world than all the people of the earth consumed in all previous history. The fact that a mere five to six per cent of mankind could and did consume in ten years more resources of the earth than all mankind in all previous ages epitomises the ecological and economic crises of our times.
> The problem is not that we have only one space craft earth, or

even that its resources are finite, but that it has a minority of first class passengers who are in a position to use and abuse its scarce resources while the majority of the passengers somehow manage to survive.

Hence the problem of mass poverty in the world today and the modern ecological crisis are the twin manifestations of the same basic malady—the irresponsible use of the scarce resources of this world by an affluent and acquisitive minority. It is this basic problem that we should confront and analyse.

Most of the first class passengers of this space craft are in a few identifiable areas. But even in the poorest parts of the world there are first class passengers who own and use the resources of their lands.

The first class passengers of the world everywhere are brought into contact through the international economy and an international civilization of their own.

. . . A common remedy suggested to solve the ecological crisis is a universal reduction of the rate of growth.

The ecological crisis can be solved only when the resources of the world can be used for producing the basic needs of life of the poor majority.

But the paradox of the situation is that the present world order can generate no power to cause such a diversion of resources.[23]

When economists are speaking boldly against the exploiting minority of first class passengers in the space craft called the earth, should we theologians keep silent on such issues and preach only on individual salvation, the good samaritan, the prodigal son and the proclamation of the gospel without even uttering the word 'classless society' because Karl Marx used it to defend the class war as a means to classless society?

I may even go a step further and claim that the *sobornost* principle of Orthodoxy maintains the classlessness and commonality of the church more than both the pyramidical hierarchy of the Roman Catholic Church and the opposite of it in the congregationalist Protestant brethren. We have to disentangle the present structures of the church and omit whatever is not in line with the family analogy of the church. If St. Thomas Aquinas defended private property, it was due to the feudalistic influence of his age. We know that the dignity of a person does not depend on his property. Our Lord has said the last word on it, 'A man's life does not consist in the

48

abundance of his possessions' (Lk. 12: 15). According to the Scriptures the whole world and the fulness thereof belongs to the Lord and we are only stewards. The steward has no ownership.

New Duties of the Church

1. If we accept social justice as of paramount importance and the creation of a world family in the model of the Holy Trinity as the ideal towards which we must constantly move with the help and guidance of the Holy Spirit till we see him as he is at the parousia, we have to unlearn many things we have learned and re-direct our steps in the right direction. The paradoxical nature of many of the doctrines is not yet fully realized.

Søren Kierkegaard rightly calls Jesus Christ the supreme paradox. The divine-humanity of the incarnation cannot be expressed in human language except in paradoxical terms because of the limitation of human languages. Therefore, it is wrong to speak of the finished work of Christ without also speaking of the unfinished appropriation of it by each and all. Similarly it is wrong to speak of justification by faith alone, without also saying in the same breath that faith without works is dead. Again, individual responsibility for salvation has to be understood in the context of the social milieu.

2. There is hardly any confession of the social sins in which we are involved as we teach only individualistic ethics in the churches. The Church of the Brethren who teach that all are brothers may have millionaire members who will be perfectly happy if they just set apart tithe for others and enjoy nine-tenths for themselves and their own children. We the Metropolitans of the Orthodox Churches have our own share of guilt in enjoying a higher standard of life than most of humanity. There is hardly a Roman Catholic or Orthodox Christian who, having built a huge private house for his small family when his neighbour is living in a leaking hut with too many children, feels so sorry for the sin he has committed that he confesses it before the Father Confessor and then builds a house for his neighbour as an atonement. As long as private

49

property is allowed, parents will give their property only to their children and they will do so with no guilt feeling, irrespective of the fact that we are enjoined to love our neighbour as ourselves.

3. 'Politics is the art of the possible.' The church must not be indifferent to the political education of her members. The churches have tolerated imperialism, feudalism, monarchy and capitalism in the past as the community conditioned the thinking of the churches. I am not saying that socialism is the panacea for all the ills of society, but it is nearer biblical teaching than capitalism and a mixed economy. It is not easy to break the iron structures of capitalistic exploitation of multi-national corporations and the underground Mafia of the underworld as well as overground Mafia of the capitalistic, economic system. We cannot, however, be silent about it any more and keep the church on the side of the establishment, the oppressor and her richer members. The prophetic voice of Amos should not be silenced by the hierarchy. It is certainly easier to practise Christianity in socialism than in capitalism, if by Christianity we mean total Christianity including God and neighbour.

4. The Bible has to be taught in home, Sunday school and church in a new way. Hardly anybody teaches the Lord's Prayer with its social implications. Do we ever note that the first person singular does not appear in it and that provision, pardon, protection and preservation are asked for the whole of humanity in it? Do we recognize or teach that the meaning of 'Give us this day our daily bread' is , 'Lord divide all the bread of all the world for all the people of all the world and give me only my share and nothing more'? We are not asked to pray for daily cake when our neighbours are not even having daily rice or dry *chapati*. Does not the invocation 'Our Father' imply that we are all brothers and sisters when we say that prayer? We are not to address God as 'Our Grandfather in heaven' and justify our interpersonal relationships as that of first cousins or second cousins.

There are many passages in the Bible which have to be taught as our Lord taught his disciples to pray this prayer which imply the brotherhood of man under the Fatherhood of God. The sharing of resources soon after Pentecost was not an

50

experiment that failed, but the fulness of the Christian church which could not be kept up in a world of Ananiases and Sapphiras (Acts 5). The Holy Spirit is now guiding the whole world into a classless society practising not only common consumption, but also common production. This is necessary owing to the delay of the promised return of the Lord. The often repeated saying of our Lord that it is more difficult for the rich man to enter the kingdom of God than for a camel to go through the eye of a needle is not to be discarded as the Hebrew hyperbole our Lord used accidentally. 'Travel light' is the principle of Christian pilgrimage on earth. He himself became poor and showed us the way to heaven, following in his footsteps, carrying our crosses. We often say that Abraham the rich is in paradise and that the rich people of today can be with him, without comparing the character and time of Abraham with our character and our time. Do the rich today show the kind of hospitality that Abraham showed to the poor wayfarers (Gen. 18)?

5. The stewardship principle which is central in the teaching of Christ is used for stewardship campaigns, usually to raise the percentage of giving to charity, but it is not taught in depth. 'The Lord God took the man and put him in the garden of Eden to till it and to keep it' (Gen. 2:15). Adam was not given the ownership of the garden. As 'God has made of one blood all nations of men to dwell on all the face of the earth' (Acts 17: 26), all are the children of God placed on this earth to till it and to keep it and not to claim ownership of it. David realized this long ago and prayed, 'Thine O Lord, is the greatness . . . for all that is in the heavens and in the earth is thine; . . . Both riches and honour come from thee and thou rulest over all . . . For all things come from thee, and of thy own have we given thee' (1 Chron. 29: 10–14). God the owner of time, talents and resources has entrusted them to us in different (Matt. 25) and equal (Luke 19) proportions and we should use them for the good of the human family which is our own family in the context of God's Fatherhood. The right to private property is not unambiguously taught in the Old Testament. Adam was expelled from the garden as he claimed ultimate right on it by disobeying the real owner. Israelites have been exiled to Egypt, Babylon and Assyria, and Palestine

was occupied by others to show that even the Holy Land belongs to God. The Jubilee Year reallotment of the land recommended in Leviticus 25 was not to assert the private claims of the original families, but to abide by the division effected by Joshua according to the commandment of God, and the Israelites failed to practise it.

Christian stewardship, which Mahatma Gandhi called trusteeship, must be taught in such a way that at least the growing generation will see the sinfulness of our inherited wealth and structures and work for a theology of a classless society. Much contemporary study of the Bible is not theologically oriented. We shall never arrive at a theology of a classless society by a subjective study which determines 'the canon within the canon' of the Bible in advance and then concentrates on such passages and proof-texts to substantiate the narrow canon which we have already accepted unconsciously, or even perhaps consciously.

A theological study of the Bible, on the other hand, does not start with adult baptism or speaking in tongues or justification by faith alone or the Protestant principle or the Catholic substance, but with the doctrine of creation, redemption, consummation or the very doctrine of the Holy Trinity which is the one distinguishing mark of the Christian revelation of God. These universally accepted doctrines of the church are not narrow canons of any particular reformer or denomination, but the faith of the one undivided church from the beginning to the end. We ignore the patristic writings at our own peril. Any study of the Scriptures which forgets the church and her venerable doctrines is self-defeating. The church whether the Old Israel or the New Israel came into being before the written Bible. The Holy Spirit is the father, and the church the mother of the Bible. The ancient and continuing doctrines of the church which are based on the Bible, but not limited by it, have to play a decisive role in any study of the Bible which is sound and uniting. The brief outline of a theology of a classless society dealt with in the next chapter is to convince the open-minded reader of this book that such a theology exists and needs detailed study by the whole church of the whole world, especially in the momentous days in which we are living.

52

6. Another need of the hour is a new approach to and dialogue with communism. Thank God that both of these have begun all over the world. Thinkers on both sides have begun to realize that a fresh approach or attitude to each other is indispensable. God, who chose Cyrus the heathen to fulfil his plans about Israel, was gracious enough to choose Karl Marx, Engels, Lenin and Mao Tse-tung to fulfil his plan to evolve a classless society. The atheism and materialism of communism are only passing phenomena as both these are untruths, and error will finally be defeated by truth. God, in his providence, is certainly guiding history.

When the communists say that there is no God, 'He who sitteth in heaven laughs'. More young people attend the churches in Russia now than 10 years ago. (Between my first visit of a month in 1967 and my recent visit in 1976 there was a marked improvement in the attendance of youth in the churches of the Soviet Union.) Communist dialecticians like Garaudi have already taken the initiative for communist-Christian dialogues with discernibly good effects. The churches have a great responsibility to respond positively without fear or prejudice as we have no need of an inferiority complex, if we believe that the lion of Judah will triumph ultimately as he has already triumphed in his cross and resurrection. A lot of the anti-communism of the church in the past was due to the vested interests of the rich within the churches and was the result more of economic than theological considerations.

Even the very question of violence is now a major topic of fresh study among Christian theologians and they have come to the conclusion that hardly anybody is non-violent in our exploiting structures of injustice in which we are all voluntarily or involuntarily involved. The alternative is not between violence and non-violence but between greater and lesser violence, between structural and special violence and between hidden and manifest violence. If we are silent about the endemic violence of the unjust economic, cultural and social structure of our society and raise a hue and cry about the bloody revolution which is the result of the former, we are justifying the evil tree and condemning only the evil fruit. An open-hearted dialogue with communist dialectitians and

53

Christian theologians is likely to deepen the insight of the church into social justice and open the hearts of the communists towards God, without whom nothing can be explained to the satisfaction of all.

7. The conscientization process needs to be stepped up in India by every means available on the initiative of the Christian churches. Paulo Freire's *The Pedagogy of the Oppressed* and the conscientization he and others are carrying out in Brazil and other countries in South America ought to be a lesson to the leaders of the Indian church. Conscientization has to start both from the top and from the bottom. The consciousness of the sense of dignity of the oppressed and the necessary pricking of the conscience of the oppressor are included in this painful process. The churches of the west which are wealthy on account of the riches their countries have accumulated by exploiting the poor countries, through their governments, multi-national corporations and unfair trade regulations, must become the accusing conscience of their governments concerning the growing gulf between the rich and the poor countries.

The rich people of India likewise are rich owing to their exploitation of the gullible poor of India. Who can deny the fact that anyone who is rich is rich because of the labour of others? The clothes we put on, the food we eat, the roads we walk on, the vehicles in which we travel, the schools and colleges where we study, the hospitals where we are treated and the riches we possess are all due to the labour of many and should make us all deeply obliged and indebted to the community, the church and the world. Therefore, it is only just and fair that all our earnings, capabilities, time and talents ought to be spent for the good of the society which makes us what we are.

Our conscience has to be Christianized or sensitized to tell us that we are robbers if we give the society's resources entrusted to us only to our own children. Christians have been given the law and the gospel in addition to the universal corrective of conscience but neither has effectively accused the animal instincts practised by the capitalistic system of the western and eastern Christian society. As St. Paul declares, 'It is not by hearing the law, but by doing it, that men will be

54

justified before God'. Concerning the Gentiles, St. Paul says that 'their conscience is called as witness, and their own thoughts argue the case on either side, against them or even for them, on the day when God judges the secrets of human hearts through Christ Jesus' (Rom. 2:15). If Jesus Christ becomes the conscience of the Christian, he will never be selfish with personal ambition for himself but will live for others.

Owing to the lack of teaching on social justice, there is hardly any corrective or accusing finger pointed against those of us who enjoy luxuries or accumulate wealth or build huge houses when our own neighbours live in squalor, misery and poverty. The change that took place in the conscience of Zacchaeus when Jesus visited his house does not take place in the conscience of the present tax-collectors, employers, ministers, estate owners, bank managers, traders and even Metropolitans though they claim to be Christians. A person who cheated the railways by travelling without a ticket may send double the price to the railways with a letter of apology, but still feel no guilt about the huge salary or income he has in a country of poverty. It was refreshing news to read in the Ecumenical Press Service about clergymen in Scandinavia who were on strike demanding a lesser salary than what they were being paid. The problem cannot be solved by the voluntary self-emptying of a few in the affluent countries or even of the highest strata of the poor countries, but only by evolving a socialistic world government which helps all to practise universal brotherhood.

A World Order for Social Justice

The one great fact of our times is that for the first time in the history of the world we have one world where all problems are cosmic and all solutions have to be of a cosmic dimension. Dietrich Bonhoeffer's discovery that man has come of age has no meaning if man has not become capable of realizing that he has to consider himself a member of the world family. It is often pointed out that the very concept of one world was never activated until Jesus Christ the cosmic person commissioned his disciples, 'Go ye unto all the world'. Only when the

Christian church and her mission became world-wide did the scientific spirit, democracy, communism and technology help to unite the world into one neighbourhood. But the two world blocks of the developed and the developing nations have not yet been united into a world order for social justice, either by the United Nations and its auxiliaries like UNCTAD or by the innumerable world bodies like the World Council of Churches and their sub-units.

In the exclusive interview that the President-elect Jimmy Carter gave to the generally right-wing *Time* magazine (15th November 1976) he is reported to have said, 'I hope to get what we call "world order" instead of power politics. World order means to me to try to establish peace'. It is gratifying that the President of the richest nation in the world, the United States of America, is realizing that there will be no peace in the world until a world order is created. In the same issue of the magazine, under *Religion,* (page 61), Dom Helder Camara, Archbishop of Olinda and Recife,is called 'the lonely voice for social justice in Brazil'. The most unhappy feature of the established church in any country is the lack of foresight of the majority of the hierarchy about the need for social justice.

Social justice does not mean communism as feared by the right-wing defenders of the *status quo*. A world order for social justice means true democracy of the people of the whole world by the representatives of the whole world for the people of the whole world. It means not only an international economic order, but a democratic, socialistic world government, egalitarianism, and a limiting of individual freedom for the good of the whole world. The cultural, educational and social revolution of the contemporary world must take the Chinese experiment for what it is worth and go beyond it to a blending together of individual initiative and the common good. It may sound utopian to expect the United Nations to usher in a world government, but it would be suicidal to continue the present national self-interest, the competitive arms race and the staggering exploitation of the poor and developing countries by the rich and the developed. The world order for social justice needs a world buffer stock of food, medicines, and a world army as a world police force.

The church must play an important role in this direction.

56

The churches of the world must stand for a theology of a classless society, a simpler life-style, absolute selflessness, all motivated by the true meaning of the specifically Christian virtue of *agape* (divine love). Love in its perfection not only aims at egalitarianism but also practises equality in opportunity. Similarly, in a world family of nations, each nation with its distinctive resources (e.g. oil-rich Arab countries, technologically advanced western nations, and Asia with its riches in raw materials) must reckon itself an equal partner in a world family. National and cultural identities would then fit in as different colours of a brilliant rainbow. Self-interest without an interest in our neighbour is the bane of our life today. We need our neighbours as our neighbours need us and so our Lord has taught us the unfailing law of survival, 'Love your neighbour as yourself'. The law of the jungle was 'kill the neighbour before he kills you'. Our present motto is 'live and let live'. The indispensable motto for tomorrow would be, 'consider your neighbour and yourself as one and live as one family'.

The capitalistic Christians are very fond of the parable of ten talents in which the one talent of the idle servant was added to the ten talents of the hard-working steward. They conveniently forget the parable of the labourer who worked only for one hour and was paid at par with the labourer who worked for six hours, on the basis of the equal need of the former (Matt. 20). In this parable, the employer is acting more like a loving father than like a shrewd employer. The Christian church has yet to learn and practise and teach that Christian love is more than charity; it is social justice. The church is often an inseparable part of the secular society in which it is placed. That society also determines the structures of the church. The difference in the living standard of the bishop, the priest and the poor layman is greater in a bourgeois capitalist society than in a socialist society. The ideal thing to do is to imitate the Lord rather than conform to the sociological pressures of our environment, but only a few individuals can do so.

The urgency of social justice has never been felt before as much as in our century and we cannot afford to ignore its centrality if the church is to survive.

4
OUTLINE OF THE THEOLOGY
OF A CLASSLESS SOCIETY

Authors more competent than I can write volumes on the theology of a classless society. In fact, all theology worth the name Christian has to be in this line. The theology of other religions also, if not perverted by sectarianism would point towards a world brotherhood. *Advaita* of Sree Sankaracharya, for example, had no place for any dualism in his teachings of Brahman, *atman* (soul) and the world. Ramanujacharya, the main exponent of *Visishtadvaita* (qualified non-dualism), considered the world as the body of Brahman and asserted a unity of humanity and God. Islam is also interested in creating a world brotherhood under an Islamic concept of the sovereignty of Allah, the ultimacy of the Quran and the finality of Mohammed. Buddhism, Jainism and Sikhism are all against casteism. Let me try, in this chapter, to see each of the major chapters of Christian theology from the standpoint of trinitarian equality and distinction within humanity.

Creation
'And God said, "Let us make man in our own image, after our likeness and let them have dominion . . . upon the earth" ' (Gen. 1:26). The image of God is trinitarian comprehending distinctions between Fatherhood, Sonship and Motherhood within the unity and the equality of God's being. (See the previous chapter on Sin and Class Formation.) 'God has made of one blood all nations of men to dwell on all the face of the earth' (Acts 17:26). Thus there is only one class in creation. It is not only one class, but one blood and one family that God originally created. The end of creation is also the logos creator, Jesus Christ, our Lord, 'for in him all things were created, in heaven and on earth, visible and invisible, whether thrones or

dominions or principalities or authorities—all things were created through him and for him. He is before all things and in him all things hold together' (Col. 1:16, 17).

Christians see the unity of humanity in creation not only in the abstract logos which all of creation shares (as the Stoics taught), but also in the concrete logos who is the Christ. The Christian churches need a deeper insight into the unity we have with humanity and nature in creation in order to realize our unity with those outside the church. The reality of the created order of existence is also an axiom of Christian theology. The world is not illusory or Maya, which cannot rebel against the creator. It is not just an emanation either, but a real created existence. It can maintain its classlessness and unity only in relation to the creator who alone holds it together. The old or first heaven and the first earth created by God will pass away only when the new heaven and the new earth will dawn in the final day (Rev. 21 ff.).

The Fall

The fall was from unity to plurality, from one family to many warring families, from one Eden, the garden of God, to the many lands of thorns and thistles. In the primitive dreaming innocence of the days of Adam, there was no fear or suspicion of fellowmen or lack of trust in God. Sin is the greatest divisive force in the world. If Cain and Abel had lived in perfect harmony, they would have been an ideal nuclear family or a classless society; but they could not do so since anyone rejected by God will automatically hate his fellowman. A common loyalty to the absolute alone can hold humanity together and the fall was a drift from loyalty to God to loyalty to satan, self and the world. All selfishness is sin and therefore divisive. One circle can have only one centre. God alone ought to be that centre. By rebellion against the will of God Adam and Eve asserted two wills, which when questioned, could not take up the responsibility of disobedience.

The fall is that condition of the self when the self loses the divine self and the human self in obedience to the devilish self. Sin takes away from the sinner the courage to be. The fall defaces the *imago Dei* and asserts the beastly nature in man. Just as the animals cannot be a classless society, so fallen man cannot move to the unity of humanity until he is redeemed from the fallen condition. The universality of class structures in the world must be attributed to the universality of sin. The fallen man has an inferiority complex which expresses itself as a superiority complex. The fallen man carries a chip on his shoulder and is over conscious of his self-dignity. He wants to be noted by others as a good person and does not recognize his own sins. His interest is not in others, but in himself, his security, pride, arrogance and self-will. He has already created a class around himself, whether it is his family or club or gang or political party or even his sectarian religion. Like Cain he wants a mark on his forehead lest others might kill him, though he has himself killed his brother Abel. He has a double standard, one for himself and his own narrow class and another for all others outside his clan or class.

The class of the fallen is always over against someone else whereas the church is a class for the whole world. The colossal expenses for armaments of the various governments of the world to be used *against* others must be contrasted with the infinitesimal expenses of the Red Cross etc. for others. There is no greater need today than the creation of a world government, but the rich countries of the world will object to it with more vehemence than the poor, because too much wealth has an ability to make one beastly. The present nationalism which asserts national sovereignty over all the international controls of a world government must at least be recognized as a result of the fall, which made man selfish and proud. Can't we light a candle rather than cursing the darkness?

Reconciliation

Redemption is reconciliation to the triune God and consequently to one another. 'For as many of you as were baptized into Christ have put on Christ. There is neither Jew nor Greek, there is neither slave nor free, there is neither male nor female, for you are all one in Christ Jesus' (Gal. 3:27f.). The breaking down of the walls is the very theme of Paul's letter to the Ephesians. To quote a famous passage from it,

> Remember that you were at that time separated from Christ, alienated from the commonwealth of Israel, and strangers to the covenants of promise, having no hope and without God in the world. But now in Christ Jesus you who once were far off have been brought near in the blood of Christ. For he is our peace, who has made us both one, and has broken down the dividing wall of hostility, by abolishing in his flesh the law of commandments and ordinances that he might create in himself one new man in place of the two, so making peace, and might reconcile us both to God in one body through the cross, thereby bringing the hostility to an end. (2:12–16.)

The classless society, the church through which the whole of humanity is to be reconciled to God,includes the living and the departed. 'For in him all the fulness of God was pleased do dwell, and through him to reconcile to himself all things, whether on earth or in heaven, making peace by the blood of his cross' (Col. 1:19f.). Those in hades are all to be brought under the lordship of Christ and so Christ descended into hades (1 Pet. 3:16ff.; 4:6). The end of *kenosis* (self-emptying) was 'that at the name of Jesus every knee should bow, in heaven and on earth and under the earth' (Phil. 2:10). It is double pity that the church is far from a classless society. A divided church is a poor missionary of classless society. Casteism and discriminations within the church are an anomaly. Feuds, quarrels and litigations between the members of a so-called reconciled community are an offence to those who are not Christians. We must confess in all humility that reconciliation is only an ongoing process and that the goal is far ahead of us. Christians and good people of other religions and no religion are not free from the marks of the fallenness of fallen humanity. We were saved by the atoning death and resurrection of Christ, we are being saved daily by the Holy Spirit and we will be saved ultimately at the second coming of the Lord. Therefore the saved are yet to be saved and the reconciled yet to be reconciled. Like St. Peter, we are following the Lord afar off. If we do not follow him more closely, a time may come when we may deny him thrice before the cock crows twice.

62

The Church

The church as the body of Christ cannot be more than one. There cannot be many classes in one body. 'There is one body and one Spirit, just as you were called to one hope that belongs to you all, one Lord, one faith, one baptism, one God and Father of us all' (Eph. 4:4f.). Similarly, one shepherd has only one sheepfold (John 10:16) and other sheep are also to be brought into the same flock. Christ the one bridegroom has only one bride, the church. 'Let us rejoice and exult and give him the glory, for the marriage of the lamb has come, and his bride has made herself ready' (Rev. 19:7). All the analogies of the church are in the singular whether vineyard (John 15), God's field and God's building (1 Cor. 3:9) or new humanity (2 Cor. 7:17 etc.). The church is the nuclear family of God consisting of God the Father, the church guided and used by the Holy Spirit the Mother, Jesus Christ the eldest eternal brother and all Christians direct brothers and sisters. As all are reborn in baptism there are only brothers and sisters in the church and no first cousins or second cousins.

The classlessness of the church is clearly indicated in the vision of the church in the eschatological dimension as recorded in Revelation 7, 'Behold, a great multitude which no man could number, from every nation, from all tribes and peoples and tongues, standing before the throne and before the lamb, clothed in white robes, with palm branches in their hands and crying out with a loud voice, "Salvation belongs to our God who sits upon the throne, and to the lamb".' All the cultural and colour distinctions are like those of a rainbow created by the prism of history and ultimately we are all to be clothed in the white robe of holiness which is our essential mark. There should be no discrimination against those who are not marked with the seal of baptism as they also bear the image of God in creation and are marked for the one, holy, catholic, apostolic church of the living God, if not in history, then beyond. 'The saying is sure and worthy of full acceptance, that Christ Jesus came into the world to save sinners' (1 Tim. 1:15). If sinners are worth dying for, they are worth living for. Therefore they also belong to our own family. The whole of humanity is the potential church. It is bad psychology to take the gospel to people who are not Christians as if they are strangers. The mistake of the priest and the levite in the parable of the Good Samaritan was that they considered the wounded co-religionist as 'a certain man', but the Good Samaritan considered him as a brother. A true churchman will be a Good Samaritan greeting even strangers as brothers. If we have the mind of Christ, our ecclesiology will be that of the master.

The Ministry

It is the concept of the royal ministry which has planted the ideology of two classes of the ruler and the ruled in the minds of many. Although our Lord was a prophet, priest and king, he was also the suffering servant who said, 'The son of man also came not to be served but to serve, and to give his life a ransom for many'. He washed the feet of the disciples to show that the master and the disciples belong to one class and must wash each other's feet (John 13). Unfortunately, the pattern of the Roman government and hierarchical structure so crept into the western church through pyramidical hierarchy and papal supremacy and infallibility that the self-accepted title of the Pope, 'Servant of the Servants of God', is not taken seriously by the church at large, nor the world. Thank God there is a new stress on collegiality from the time of the Second Vatican Council and let us pray that the trinitarian collegial hierarchical structure will be accepted by the Pope also in the near future. The meaning of the highpriestly prayer of our Lord, 'that they may all be one; as thou, Father art in me, and I in thee, that they also may be in us, so that the world may believe that thou hast sent me' (John 17:21) is not yet fathomed by the hierarchy itself. Our Lord has shown us that the model for hierarchy and the church is the Holy Trinity. The world will believe in Jesus Christ only when the Pope gives up the claims of supremacy and infallibility and the right to veto the decisions of the ecumenical councils and acts as the servant of the servants of God, with no veto power. The only infallible guide for the church can be God, the triune, present in the church as the indwelling Holy Spirit and so even the infallibil-
64

ity of the whole church is on the basis of the dictum of the first Council of Jerusalem, that 'it has seemed good to the Holy Spirit and to us' (Acts 15:28). The very word 'minister' implies the royalty of service.

Any disciplining done by the bishop or Pope is only like that of a father to children and not of a secular king to subjects as it was in the Roman government. The father is not a class different from the children. The way of addressing the bishop as 'my lord' must also change to 'my father' if the theology of the classless society is taken seriously. The lord and the slave belong to two classes, but not the father and the children. The central revelation of the New Testament about God by his eternal Son is not God's lordship, but his fatherhood. Even if we compare Jesus Christ to the head, the Holy Spirit to the heart and the ministry to the veins, arteries and the nervous system, all of them are in one person and so in one class. The special ministry of the church is within the church and not above it.

The church has a ministry within and the church as a whole has a ministry to the world. 'You are a chosen race, (and not many races), a royal priesthood (of all the believers) a holy nation (and not many nations), God's own people (not many peoples), that you may declare the wonderful deeds of him who called you out of darkness into the marvellous light' (1 Pet. 2:9). There is of course, a special threefold ministry of *episkopos, presbuteros* and *diakonos,* but they are not three classes in distinction without unity. All the baptized belong to the royal priesthood but among them there are different degrees of grace and distinct functions for each of the special ministries. As deacon Philip had no right to lay hands and give confirmation. Peter and John had to come to Samaria for the laying of hands on the baptized, but that did not mean that the apostles were an entirely different class.

The theology of a classless society, therefore, has to be made meaningful by a simpler life-style of the ministers whether they are popes or patriarchs or bishops or priests, district superintendents or pastors. It is the church that must manifest a socialist pattern of a sustainable and living standard for all the rulers and the ruled. There is more of a Christian theological basis in the practical egalitarian society of modern China than in the western and eastern churches of our time. The need to Christianize the Chinese people is not greater than the need to Christianize the western churches. Let us pray the Holy Spirit to continue the mission in the whole world according to the need of each country.

Sacramental Theology

Sacraments are a visible means of invisible grace. The purpose of sacraments is the divinization of the church and Christians. Sacraments set apart the participants into a mystical unity from the paganized and demonized world of mutual hatred and quarrels. Holy baptism is the rite of initiation to the unity and sanctity of the church, and the baptismal water is the womb of the mother church and those who are physically given birth from many wombs are spiritually regenerated from one womb to make them one nuclear family. The holy oil (*muron*) of confirmation is the sacrament of the anointment of the one Holy Spirit to make the baptized a spiritual community. They are no more their own, but the possession of the Paraclete, to be guided and used by the self-same Spirit as various limbs of the same body.

The holy eucharist is the sacrament that perfects all sacraments, and by receiving the body and blood of Christ we are united to Christ the head to do his will as his organs in his body, the church. According to St. Paul, if there are divisions among us, it is not the Lord's supper that we eat. Unity in faith alone would not make us one. How can one organ of the body be lean and another fat and then call itself the body of Christ? 'When you meet together, it is not the Lord's supper that you eat. For in eating, each one goes ahead with his own meal, and one is hungry and another is drunk. What! Do you not have houses to eat and drink in? Or do you despise the church of God and humiliate those who have nothing?' (1 Cor. 11:20–22). The holy eucharist is for those who have an intimate sharing fellowship which prompts them to share the material wealth also with those with whom they communicate. An African friend at the Nairobi Assembly shouted, 'In our culture, the brothers eat together; and if we do not eat

66

together, we are not brothers'. He is perfectly right. Brothers share the father's property alike and the members of the church must share the Father's property alike before they share in the body and blood of Christ. There is no depth in the intercommunion practised today. Communion is a *koinonia* and must be so practised and the class–structured church has no right to communicate together.

Confession whether auricular or public is to be followed by absolution, whereby one has been reconciled to God and to our fellowmen. Matthew 5:23–25 must be brought to the attention of those who come to the confessional that none might receive the holy eucharist before reconciliation with his brother or sister. True confession is to purify the Christian and to deepen his unity with others. Holy matrimony is not a human contract but God uniting the two into one body from the moment the sacrament is performed and the couple have consummated the sacrament in God's providence. Ordination, though like marriage, is not obligatory for all; it is a sacrament of special grace for those who have a specialized vocation. But as already pointed out in the section on the ministry, the ordained belong to the unity of the church and are not a distinct class without solidarity with the church. The anointing of the sick is not extreme unction among the Orthodox churches, but a sacrament for the healing of disease by the healing oil, as practised in the early church (James 5:14).

The sacraments are not limited to 7 and we have sacraments for the dedication of the church, houses etc. All sacraments of the church are to unite the participants in the unity of the mystical body. Class distinctions and sacraments cannot go together.

The Holy Trinity

As will be noted again and again in this book, Trinity is the hall-mark of Christianity and its central theology of a classless society. Emil Brunner is wrong when he says that the Trinity is not to be preached, only to be worshipped. The Fathers of the church, who knew that the mystery of Trinity can only be adored and not scrutinized, spent their whole lives explaining its mystery. Christianity need not be apologetic about the doctrine of the Trinity, but let us praise the Lord for having revealed it to us through the incarnation and pentecost. Trinity is the mystery of God's perfection and eternal love. God does not lack singularity or plurality, nor simplicity or complexity, nor infinity or finitude in his perfection. If he is a monad, he cannot be eternal love in eternal action. If he is just a diad, there is only mutuality and reciprocity like that of a married couple, but no common sharing of love in a child and all the dimensions of love. Trinity is the greatest truth about God revealed to us by God alone. God has either to be a *Nirguna Brahma* (Attributeless Absolute) as taught by Sankara or he has to be Trinity, which means 'God is love' in all eternity. There is no dimension of love which a quadranity would include which Trinity does not consist of.

One of the main insights of the Cappadocian Fathers about the Trinity is his co-equality, co-essentiality and co-eternity. Love in its perfection has no question of greater and smaller, superior or inferior. Co-inherence (*perichoresis*) teaches that where the Father or the Son or the Holy Spirit works, all work. The Father is not older than the Son and the Spirit. In a perfect family none is isolated from the other two persons either in sorrow or in joy. The sun's heat and rays are inseparable. It is not tritheism to say that God is a nuclear family because the family of God is an ontological singularity. The human mind is a unity as well as a unit though there is the unconscious mind, the subconscious mind and the conscious mind in one. As no analogy in the created order can convey the whole depth of the mystery of Trinity, the example of the nuclear family has the shortcoming of the older father and younger son, but such Arian sub-numeration is not implied in the orthodox teaching.

The ideal of the classless society of Godhead is not attainable in history, but it can be kept as the model and appropriated as closely as possible. The distinctions are necessary even in the Godhead. The five fingers are distinct in size and usefulness, but they have a solidarity and unity which a classless society also can have. The primacy of the father is as first among equals (*primus inter pares*). The primacy of Peter in the apostolic college was also as first among equals. As the oldest of the group, he had a special honour, but no authority which was his alone. If he were given the keys of the kingdom to bind and to loose, so also were the others (Matt. 18:18; John 20:22). All the apostles were to carry on the kingly, priestly and the pastoral functions of the Lord, 'As the Father has sent me, even so I send you'.

The argument of St. Paul in Galatians 2 is to point out his equality with St. Peter and the freedom we have in Christ.

> And from those who were reputed to be something (Peter?) (what they were makes no difference to me; God shows no partiality)—those, I say, who were of repute added nothing to me; but on the contrary, when they say that I had been entrusted with the gospel to the uncircumcised, just as Peter had been entrusted with the gospel to the circumcised (for he who worked through Peter for the mission to the circumcised worked through me also for the Gentiles), and when they perceived the grace that was given to me, James and Cephas and John, who were reputed to be pillars, gave to me and Barnabas the right hand of fellowship, that we should go to the Gentiles and they to the circumcised; only they would have us remember the poor, which very thing I was eager to do. (2:6–10.)

In the following passage we see St. Paul opposing St. Peter to his face, because he stood condemned. We see no infallibility for St. Peter here or anywhere in the Scriptures except the infallibility of the revealed truth which he confessed, namely, that Jesus Christ is the Son of the living God. Even here, it was not flesh and blood which revealed it to him, but the Father in heaven (Matt. 16:16–20). It was the disciples who were strictly charged in v.20 to tell no one that he was the Christ. Trinitarian theology does not allow any pyramidical hierarchy, but only collegiality and equality of the apostles. If one is above the others, a classless theology is impossible.

Eschatology

Our final hope is not first class, second class and third class, but the Father's house. 'In my Father's house there are many rooms . . . and when I go and prepare a place for you, I will come again and will take you to myself, that where I am you may be also' (John 14:2–3). 'Beloved, we are God's children now; it does not yet appear what we shall be, but we know that when he appears we shall be like him, for we shall see him as he is' (1 John 3:2). Thank God that the many rooms are in the one house of the Father. Heaven will be the perfect classless society.

The song of the four living creatures and the twenty-four elders and of all the saints of God before the crucified and risen lamb of God is concerning the unity effected by the lamb, 'Worthy art thou to take the scroll and to open its seals, for thou wast slain and by thy blood didst ransom men for God from every tribe and tongue and people and nation, and hast made them a kingdom and priests to our God, and they shall reign on earth' (Rev. 5:9f.). It is significant that the song is not about 'pie in the sky, bye and bye, when you die', but 'they shall reign on earth'. Christianity has the hope of a new heaven and a new earth when our old world will pass away with its dividing seas and oceans. The marks of the new heaven are the marks of a perfect paradise, 'Behold, the dwelling of God is with men. He will dwell with them and they shall be his people, and God himself will be with them; he will wipe away every tear from their eyes, and death shall be no more, neither shall there be mourning, nor crying nor pain any more, for the former things have passed away' (Rev. 21:3–4). Our daily prayer 'Thy kingdom come on earth as it is in heaven' is now answered. We see here only God and his people wiping every tear from each other's eyes. The bleeding of the lamb and the feeding of the sheep should continue until the shepherd comes again.

5
THE REALITY OF SIN AND CLASS WAR

Dr. Robert MacAfee Brown was attacked by many when he produced the thesis at the Nairobi Assembly that Jesus Christ divides before he unites. The theme of the Assembly, 'Jesus Christ frees and unites' could have been dealt with by him saying that 'sin divides and Christ unites'. Slavery and divisions are not the work of Christ, but the work of satan. The passage which Dr. Brown took as the basis for his thesis that Christ divides before he unites, 'do not think that I have come to bring peace on earth; I have not come to bring peace, but a sword. For I have come to set a man against his father, and a daughter against her mother . . .' (Matt. 10:34f.), needs interpretation in the light of the person and work of Christ as God-man.

'God is light and in him there is no darkness at all'. Darkness, divisions, hatred, sin etc. cannot come from God directly. We have the promise of the master, 'Peace I leave with you, my peace I give to you' (John 14:27) which must be seen as the work of Christ, and the sword he spoke of as what he permits in a sinful order. Class war in a family takes place when the members who take the discipleship of Christ are hated and persecuted by those who would not follow him. 'Let no one say when he is tempted, "I am tempted by God"; for God cannot be tempted with evil and he himself tempts no one; but each person is tempted when he is lured and enticed by his own desire' (James 1:13f). The Lord who created everything and found everything that he created to be very good could not have created satan directly. Hence the ancient churches have the theory of fallen angels to show that the misuse of freedom by the good angels made them devils and God did not create the devils. The possibility of ascent and descent is given to man with the image of God, as to the angels. Misuse of freedom makes him satanic and good use of his divine freedom to do the will of God makes him divine. In the fallen order in which we live, God permits class war to create a classless society since the freedom God has given to man has to be honoured even when that freedom is not submitted to the will of God.

Power and Powerlessness

The Magnificat is a song of high revolution. It shows how the power of man is checked by God in history when he gave power to the powerless. 'He has put down the mighty from their thrones, and exalted those of a low degree' (Luke 1:52). The moneyed class does not remain as the highest stratum of society for ever, nor the rulers remain rulers for ever. Parliamentary democracy has acted as a mighty weapon for dethroning corrupt governments by a peaceful revolution through the ballot box. The books of Judges and Kings are full of incidents of the overthrow of the powerful by the powerless, strengthened and guided by the presence of God through the ark of the covenant. When the Israelites become powerful and proud, they are also punished by being subjected to the persecution of powerful nations. World history is a history of wars between one class and another or between one nation and another or between allies and allies and the end result is often the overthrow of the arrogant and the powerful by the powerless all the way down to the Vietnam war. History is the story of God's wonderful actions in the world.

James Cone and the proponents of Black Theology and Liberation Theology have a point in saying that God is on the side of the oppressed and not on the side of the oppressor. God gives power to the powerless, which is mightier than the power of the powerful. The dictatorship of the proletariat of which Karl Marx speaks is not to be seen as the natural flow of history but the providential hand of God, who chooses the weak to confound the strong and uses the foolish to confound the wise. Power and might belong to God. The pale Galilean is conquering the world. The meek are inheriting the earth again and again though the powerful capture it for a short time. When some king wanted a clear proof for the existence of God, the wise minister answered, 'The Jews, my Lord'. There has been no people in history who have become so powerless and so powerful time and again. They were chosen by God to be a blessing for all the families of the earth (Gen. 12:3), but they wanted to be an exclusive powerful class and so were hated by all classes of people.

The Christian church should learn a lesson from the old Israel and share her power with the powerless lest she lose her God-given powers, whether that is the power of the Spirit or of matter. The powerlessness of the cross was able to conquer the power of the Roman Empire and continues to conquer the world by the power of service. 'For the word of the cross is folly to those who are perishing, but to us who are being saved it is the power of God . . . We preach Christ crucified, a stumbling block to Jews and folly to Gentiles, but to those who are called, both Jews and Greeks, Christ the power of God and the wisdom of God. For the foolishness of God is wiser than men, and the weakness of God is stronger than men' (1 Cor. 1:18–25).

Sin makes the powerful selfish, oppressive and exploitative. On the other hand, if we have the mind of Christ, we will not want to hold on to power, but empty ourselves of our power and stoop down to the lowest level of powerlessness to give power to the powerless (Phil. 2:5–11). As humanity at large cannot be expected to have the mind of Christ, the power of the powerful will not be parted with voluntarily. Hence the powerless must be aided by those who stand for a classless society to consolidate their power in such a way that they can exert power on the powerful through collective bargaining, strikes etc. The government which stands for justice can help also in the creation of a classless society through laws that would raise the standard of living for the poor and bring down the salary of the highly paid. Trade union leaders are often so corrupt that they take bribes from the rich owners of estates and factories and use their power for their own advantage without using it for the powerless. The leaders of the church are also guilty of identifying themselves with the moneyed class and perpetuating the class structures of the society and the churches. The church, following in the footsteps of the Nazarene, must become poor and preach the gospel to the poor, not only in words, but also in liberating them from the oppression of the mighty.

Class and Classlessness

The richest and the poorest are the least concerned for God in the class structured society. The former are too busy and the latter too indifferent. Man is a social being and so creates class structures for security, combat and prestige. A classless society as a world community can only remain an ideal on account of cultural differences, pride of nationalism and ethnic identities. Karl Marx's theory that class war would lead to a classless society and a utopia on earth fails to take seriously the sin of man. The state will not wither away as prophesied by Marx. A perfect classless society is only an eschatological possibility.

It is the image of God in man that desires a world brotherhood, a sharing of resources, world government, jobs for all, equality of opportunity, eradication of poverty and exploitation, all of which are the marks of a classless society. The fallenness, frailty and sin of man, on the other hand, make him desire his own prosperity, class formation for narrow ends, fights between classes, colossal waste of money for armaments of the most sophisticated type and a using of the lower classes for his own higher class comforts and luxuries. Man is an amphibian, living and moving towards the heights of heaven in ideas and drifting towards the depth of hell in practice. The impracticability of the theology of a classless society is because of the beast in man. Its practicability, however, is constantly hoped for since we know that the image of God is not completely lost. If man is a lump of sin as taught by Augustine, it is impossible even to dream of a classless society. But God is still on the throne and he is already bringing about some sort of a socialism all over the world, whether it is through benevolent capitalism or Russian communism or Chinese communism or through the thinking of the intelligentsia.

The Seat of Sin

Is private property the root of all evil? Is it not because of the selfishness of man that primitive communism did not last long and that slavery, feudalism and capitalism emerged in history? Sin is not to be pinpointed in the individual alone, nor in society alone, but in the cosmic evil at work in both. Sin will not disappear from the world when the whole world is brought under communism as Marx expected. All economic, cultural, social, political and even religious orders are tainted with sin. Structural injustice forces the individual to acquiesce the injustice. The reality of sin has to be discovered by introspection and by sociological studies. No 'ism' is free of sin and the possibility of corruption. The advantage of a classless society is that endemic injustice will be less there than in a capitalistic society. The inevitability of the class war was taught by Marx.

Will the dictatorship of the proletarian class, achieved by class struggle, usher in the classless society we envisage? The classless society we dream of is not the dictatorship of any class, but a democratic, socialistic rule based on a parliamentary system in which, when the party in power gets corrupted by sin and selfishness, the opposition party can come into power. The destiny of humanity cannot be entrusted to any one single party for ever as every man is a sinner. As Lord Acton said, 'Power tends to corrupt and absolute power corrupts absolutely'. 'Jesus did not trust himself to them because he knew all men and needed no one to bear witness of man; for he himself knew what was in man' (John 2:24f.). Democracy is possible because of the dignity of man, but it must be democracy with an opposition party because of the frailty of man. The fact of sin necessitates mutual corrective in every human situation. The universality of sin gives us the warning that the renewal of humanity is indispensable even in the days of the world government and classless society.

Anything outside and rebelling against the sovereignty of God is liable to corruption and decay. The Fatherhood of God is not to be a slogan which does not carry any weight, but the basic principle of life, on the basis of which all his resources are shared for all his children everywhere. Sin is that which does not take God's Fatherhood seriously. 'If any one says, "I love God," and hates his brother, he is a liar; for he who does not love his brother whom he has seen, cannot love God whom he has not seen' (1 John 4:20). The lack of love, justice and holiness is the seat of sin. Sin is Godlessness and brotherlessness. Therefore, even class war should not be out of hatred, but out of the burning desire to bring down the mighty from their thrones and exalt those of a low degree.

Priority of Soul?

In Hinduism what is all important is the supreme self (*paramatman*) and the personal self (*atman*). Thinkers of eminence like Plato, Sankara, Søren Kierkegaard and A. N. Whitehead have all subscribed to this theory in one way or another. K. Guru Dutt, a spokesman for conservative Hinduism, concludes his critical review of *Man and the Universe of Faiths* by M. M. Thomas thus, 'Kierkegaard stressed that religion was the concern of the "single one". In our own times A. N. Whitehead has said, "Religion is what a man does with his solitariness". Social activity is necessary but not primary. Today it looks as if the tail is trying to wag the dog' (*Religion and Society*, Bangalore, September 1976).

My contention in this book is that the personal and the social are inseparable and neither has priority over the other. The soul exists in body and mind and there is no priority for a disembodied soul if it exists as a separate monad. The social is not the tail and the person the dog, nor the individual the tail and the social activity the dog. Sociology which stresses the importance of sociological pressure on each individual, and individualistic psychology which emphasises the power of the mind are two complementary truths to be taken together. God does not exist as a monad because God is eternal love. The solution of the human predicament is not in *advaita* where love has no ontological nature, nor in *dwaita* which sees two entities as two eternal separate realities, but in Trinity in which love is ontological, eternal, equalizing fellowship. No person in isolation from God and fellowman can do anything.

Even Sankara does not see any salvation for *jivatma* apart

from identity with *paramatma*. We must go on to say that *jivatma* has an identity with distinction with other souls as well as with God, the triune. 'No man is an island.' Would any person learn a language if there were no other persons to communicate with? Every person is a sociological reality, a co-being being, just as God is triune. If Martin Luther had said, 'Here we stand', instead of 'Here I stand' and had a concern for the church equal to his concern for the freedom of the Christian, capitalism would not have come into existence. Personal dignity and human rights about which we hear so much, are only one side of the coin. Why should the rich alone have dignity and right without extending the same to the millions of slum-dwellers and the downtrodden? Any dignity, right or freedom I want for myself without wanting it for my neighbour also is shallow, superficial and transient. In Christian theology and ethics, I as a soul do not exist without my body and soul. Hence the Christian hope of resurrection of the body is the transformation of the carnal body to a spiritual body. We do not believe in the immortal soul, but in the resurrection of the person and the new humanity. Sin exists in the person and in the class together.

On Taming the Class War

There are thinkers who teach that a world government can never come into existence unless a world conqueror comes forward and conquers the whole world. There are also prophets of gloom who discard the whole idea as wishful thinking. More in number are the prophets of doom who expect a third or fourth world war destroying life on our tiny earth. Fundamentalistic Christian sects do not have any optimism about our world except in the apocalyptic second coming of Christ and the millennium of peace he would inaugurate on earth. Some of us, however, believe that the Holy Spirit is a present reality, not only in the church, but also in the world, 'convincing the world of sin and of righteousness and of judgement' (John 16:8). It is the same Holy Spirit who is telling the world through the scientists that the resources of the world must be used with a sense of stewardship and that a sacramental view of nature is indispensable. The rich nations of the world are becoming more and more convinced that at least a part of their wealth has come from the markets of the poor and developing Third World and that they themselves cannot make any progress unless they take the developing world along with them. UNCTAD and other United Nations agencies are asking for better 'trade and aid' rules to bridge the gulf between the 'have's' and the 'have not's'. The enlightened consciences of the rich countries of the world are also clamouring for a world government, international economic order, a cutting short of the arms race and the rechannelling of military expenses for the clearing of slums and creating employment opportunities. The wrath of many has been turned against the unpardonable exploitation of the wealth of the poor countries by the international corporations and indeed against the whole capitalistic system itself.

If we are to create a classless society three levels of force are possible—the moral, the legal and the military. Many say that the first will take a long time as the preaching of Christian love for the past 2,000 years and that of Hinduism for 7,000 years and of Buddhism and Jainism for 2,500 years have not created a just world with social justice. The legal machinery of each country is also not moving fast to create a new society. Thus many young people are impatient and are asking for a bloody revolution, military intervention and the aggravation of the class war. Religious and moral forces therefore have to be strengthened through word as well as deed. Sermons and books alone will not be sufficient. Classless communities of sharing work and reward must grow up in large numbers all over the world. Such communities must also inspire governments to create quickly rules favouring a classless society. Bloody class war will become inevitable if these two forces do not act well and act quickly. Sharing communities can tame the class war that is in the offing. Political action for a classless society must be stepped up. The church and good people must identify themselves with the oppressed, the downtrodden and the lowest strata of society and hasten the conscientization process to give them a sense of dignity and worth.

We cannot have infinite material progress in a finite world. Let us therefore be satisfied with the minimum comforts and live simply so that the poor may simply live. This alone will tame class war.

6

BY ALL, BOTH SINGLY
AND IN COMMON

The title of this chapter is a phrase from St. Athanasius. In section 5 of his famous *The Incarnation of the Word,* he speaks of the effect of the fall and adds, 'All kinds of iniquities were performed by all, both singly and in common'. Elsewhere he points out Jesus Christ alone could be the Saviour of all. To quote, 'His part it was, and his alone, both to bring again the corruptible to incorruption and to maintain for the Father his consistency of character with all. For he alone, being word of the Father and above all, was in consequence both able to recreate all, and worthy to suffer on behalf of all and to be an ambassador for all with the Father' (section 7). It seems to me that we are only beginning to realize in this moon age which started on 21st July 1969, that both the failures and achievements of man are 'both singly and in common'.

The bane of old Roman Catholicism was its stress on 'in common' when speaking of the church and on 'singly' when speaking of the Pope. The present emphasis on collegiality is a praiseworthy effort to bring individuality in line with sociality without surrendering either and at the same time maintaining both. The bane of past Protestantism was its over-emphasis on individuality without a corresponding emphasis on the doctrine of the church. The fact is that even the ultra-individualistic sectarian groups exist in groups and not in personal isolation. The first sentence uttered by the first man to step on the moon is relevant to the topic we are discussing, 'That is one small step for a man, one giant step for mankind'.

My theme is that individualization and participation are indispensable bi-polar aspects of Godhead, manhood, the church, ministry, sacraments, the world and consummation

81

of history in the kingdom of God. Here I see Athanasian theology supporting the classless society.

God as triune is the model of perfect individuality and sociality. As St. Basil says, 'What is number in the Godhead?' Trinity is not a quantitative definition of God, but a qualitative revelation of the fullness of Godhead. In one of his Letters (VIII. 2) St. Basil says, 'Against those who cast it in our teeth that we are tritheists, let it be answered that we confess one God not in number, but in nature. For everything which is called one in number is not one absolutely nor yet simple in nature; but God is universally confessed to be simple and not composite'.[24] Furthermore, in his famous treatise on the Holy Spirit he says that God is beyond number, 'But O wisest sirs, let the unapproachable be altogether above and beyond number, as the ancient reverence of the Hebrews wrote that unutterable name of God in peculiar characters, thus endeavouring to set forth its infinite excellence'.[25] The simplicity and perfection of the Godhead is in his tri-unity comprehending plurality and singularity in the ontological simplicity of love. God is Co-Being Being and in his unity there is not only potentiality but also the actuality of giving, receiving and sharing. The circle of love is complete with these three dimensions; all other dimensions are included in these.

God is both a simple monad as well as an absolute triad just as the human mind is both simple and triple. Trinity, the mark of orthodoxy, the mystery *par excellence*, is the truth behind all truths. Our theme 'singly and in common' is vindicated most clearly in the revelation of God as one and three at the same time. The Greek word *perichoresis,* translated as co-inherence, shows how each of the three persons in the one person participates in the other two in creation, redemption and providence. Trinity is both essential, stressing the unity in essence and economic, stressing the distinction of persons. God is indivisible, without part and passions and yet in his simplicity there is nothing lacking whether of singularity or plurality. We would never have known the unknowable nature of God as triune if Christ the Son had not revealed this mystery to us. Jesus Christ, the focus of God, the proper name of God, the concreteness of God, is indispensable to view God as he is, for 'only through God can God be known'.

We can seek to go further than the Cappadocian Fathers, with the never failing help of the Holy Spirit who continues to guide us to full truth and explain how the one *ousia* or essence is related to the three *hypostases* or persons in the depth of Godhead. This help comes from modern analogies like the threefold mind exposed by Freudians and depth psychology, or through other discoveries of sociology, but we must realize at the same time that the created world's analogies are inadequate to explain the creator. The principle of 'singly' in Unitarianism or Socinianism cannot stand the test of sociology, the keyword of which is 'in common', and by the same count tritheism is mistaken as it does not incorporate in the Godhead the eternity of love which in its totality constitutes the three as one. The unattainable goal, 'Be ye therefore perfect even as your heavenly Father is perfect', is still in front of us beckoning us to the length, breadth and height of love which expresses itself eternally by giving, receiving and sharing; the fullness of individualization and participation, which constitute personality.

Man and Manhood

Was the image of God given to Adam alone or to Adam and Eve together? The whole verse is thus, 'Let us make man in our image, after our likeness and let them have dominion . . . So God created man in his own image; in the image of God he created him; male and female he created them' (Gen. 1:26f.). Man is able to have dominion over the moon, Mars etc, as he is created in the image of God which is that additional faculty that distinguishes him from the subhuman species, whether it is his quest for and response to the infinite, or his ultimate freedom or his abstract reasoning or his divinity or his personality. The image or likeness, even in the Genesis narrative, before the revelation of the Trinity was singly and in common in Godhead as well as in man. Significantly 'our' and 'his' are used for God in verse 26 and 'him' and 'them' are used for man in verse 27. God is not God without singularity and plurality, and man is not man without both. The image of God was in the triune God and it was given to Adam alone, to Eve alone and to them in common. *Kamala the Wolf Child* could not develop personality alone and she developed beastly features in the company of the wolves.

There is no personality without inter-personal relationships and yet each person is distinct from every other person. The image of God in man is both a gift as well as an achievement. It is a gift reserved for man alone. Though the potentiality of *imago Dei* is a divine gift, the actualization of it is in encounter with other persons. This distinction between potentiality and actuality is not in God as he is beyond both. God as God does not grow as he is eternally perfect as life and spirit, being and becoming, static and dynamic. Man as man grows with society, society changes in accordance with the leadership of individuals. Capitalism and socialism pleading for individual freedom and social justice respectively ought to condition each other to realize the image of God given to the individual and to society together. Let us hope that both these systems will evolve into a better responsible society combining parliamentary democracy and economic justice.

The sin of man is also both personal and collective. Eve's fall was together with that of Adam. 'So when the woman saw that the tree was good for food, and that it was a delight to the eyes, and that the tree was to be desired to make one wise, she took of its fruit and ate; and she also gave some to her husband, and he ate. Then the eyes of both were opened, and they knew that they were naked' (Gen. 3:6f.). Adam is not a proper name in Hebrew but the common name meaning 'man'. The Adamic fall was both a personal and a corporate fall, like that of Goliath against David. Every individual who sins is responsible for sinning and so deserves punishment even though there may be social influences or factors of heredity that caused him to do it. As E. J. Bicknell says, 'Mankind is one in sin . . . A purely individual human life is an impossibility. If "original sin" seems unfair, we need to remember that the good tendencies and good dispositions of our nature come down to us by inheritance as well as its deficiencies. The unity of race that conditions original sin, conditions also salvation through Christ' (39 Articles, page 182). St. Athanasius was emphatic in pointing out that the Adamic fall had caused corruption of the human race, which

84

repentance would not or could not heal. Christ alone could recreate humanity that was corrupted by the individual and the corporate sin of mankind (*De Incarnatione,* 7).

The Second Vatican Council's best document, the Pastoral Constitution on the Church in the Modern World, has wisely pointed out,

> Man's social nature makes it evident that the progress of the human person and the advantage of society itself hinge on one another. For the beginning, the subject and the goal of social institutions is and must be the human person, which for its part and by its very nature stands completely in need of social life . . . To be sure the disturbances which so frequently occur in the social order result in part from the natural tensions of economic, political and social forms. But at a deeper level they flow from man's pride and selfishness, which contaminate even the social sphere (Section 25).

So what we need to aim at is not only socialization, but also the redemption of individual persons. We need to form new structures of society wherein the individual can grow in his full dimension as early as possible.

The Church, Ministry and Sacraments

The church and the Christian must be viewed 'both singly and in common'. Vladimir Lossky observes 'Thus, man is at one and the same time a part, a member of the body of Christ by his nature, but also (considered as a person) a being who contains all within himself'.[26] He says again, 'In truth we are not here concerned with individuals and with collectivity but with human persons who can only attain to perfection with the unity of nature. Pentecost is the affirmation of the multiplicity of persons within the church'.[27] The Fathers regarded the church as the image of the Holy Trinity. To Gregory of Nyssa, 'Christianity is an imitation of the divine nature'. The primacy of the hierarchy within the church ought to be understood as the primacy of the Father within the Godhead and not as heathen kingly authority.

The cardinal ideas of co-equality, co-essentiality and co-eternity are not irreconcilable with the hierarchical order in the solidarity of the church. To quote J. Meyendorff, 'The sacramental nature of the true life in the Spirit presupposes the existence of a visible church with a hierarchy possessing special functions and a charisma to teach, but it also means that the saints are authentic witnesses of the actual presence of God in the midst of his people. By means of its hierarchical and sacramental structure, the church expresses the permanence and reality of the union brought about, in Christ, between human and the divine'.[28] The unity and catholicity of the church are as important characteristics of the bride of Christ as her holiness and apostolicity, and all these four marks have a depth as well as a width individually and collectively. The ecumenical attitude of each Christian is necessary for the church's ecumenicity. Similarly the holiness of the Christian has to manifest the holiness of the church. There is also an intimate connection between the threefold particular ministry of bishop, priest and deacon and the general ministry of those baptized and anointed by the holy oil, which, according to Father Bulgakov of the Russian Church, is the ordination of the laity. Each minister singly and the church in common perpetuate the true ministry of Jesus Christ, the head.

The validity of the sacraments also has a personal as well as an ecclesiastical dimension. The theory of *ex opere operantis* shows the former, the need of the right interior attitude of the recipient, and *ex opere operato* shows the efficacy of the sacrament objectively in the right performance with the right words by the valid ministry in the church. The conclusion of such an enquiry would be that we cannot escape from the principle of 'both singly and in common' in the life of the church, a mystical union of Christians to the incarnate head in the power of the Holy Spirit.

I am trying to call those who have been fascinated by the recent trend in many parts of the world to the idea of 'churchless Christianity' to the inescapability of the church. One reason for the ineffectiveness of V. Chakkarai and P. Chenchian, two of the pioneers who wanted an indigenous theology in India, was their polemic against the church. Even Sadhu Sundar Singh, who was baptized as an Anglican but later surrendered his preacher's licence, wanted to belong to Christ without belonging to any church. He wrote, 'It is quite natural that no form of church service can ever satisfy

86

deeply spiritual people, because such persons already have direct fellowship with God in meditation, and they are always conscious of his blessed presence in their souls'.[29]

There are many all over the world today who are too individualistic to see the need of corporate worship. But true worship is both singly and in common. The church is 'the home of the faithful and the school of the saints'. Gregory Nazianzus has called the church 'the mighty body of Christ' (*On the Great Athanasius,* page 7). 'As the people of God', writes Karl Rahner, 'socially and juridically organized, the church is not a mere eternal welfare institute, but the continuation of the perpetual presence of the task and function of Christ in the economy of redemption, his contemporaneous presence in history, his life, the church in the full and proper sense'.[30] Again, 'Viewed in relation to the sacraments, the church is the primal and fundamental sacrament'.[31] The Fathers have spoken of the church as the mother, as God is the Father (cf. Gal. 4:26).

Even Chenchiah, who wrote, 'Christianity took the wrong gradient when it left the kingdom of God for the church', nevertheless advocates the need of ashrams in the Hindu model where small communities would live happily under a guru. It is an indirect admission of the necessity of a group for the growth of the individual. Is there any guarantee that ashrams would not degenerate into worldliness, if that is the charge against the church? The Lord of the church has said that 'the gates of hell shall be demolished by the church'. The Hindu emphasis on individual contemplation and the mystic realization of the identity of *jivatman* with *paramatman* needs to be supplemented by the counter emphasis on corporate worship in the church. Thank God, P. D. Devanandan, and Bishop A. J. Appaswamy have not gone the radical route taken by Chakkarai and Chenchaiah, but appreciated the need of an ecclesiology and thus subscribed to the principle of 'both singly and in common' as we have been applying in various spheres.

To Sum Up All Things in Christ

The perfection of 'singly and in common' is not in history but beyond history, in 'the new heaven and the new earth' where 'dwelleth righteousness'. The Pauline idea of recapitulation (*anakephalaiosis*) developed by St. Ireneus is that God's plan for the fulness of time is to unite all things in heaven and on earth in Jesus Christ (Eph. 1:10). Ultimate redemption beyond history is also both personal and social. Reuben would not be welcome to the place of Joseph unless Benjamin were with him (Gen. 43:5). In the same way, when Jesus sits on the throne, we cannot appear before him for reward in isolation, leaving our own brothers and sisters outside. So the words of Joseph to the elder brothers, 'Unless your youngest brother comes down with you, you shall see my face no more', is pregnant with meaning. One great saint of God once said that heaven would not be heaven for him while his brothers remained in hell and so he would rather go to hell and try to convert them and enjoy the satisfaction thereof than remain in heaven alone while others were in agony. If we believe that 'God has made of one blood all nations of men to dwell on all the face of the earth' (Acts 17:26) then certainly those in hell are also our brothers.

Furthermore, can we truthfully say that we are not respons-ible for sending them to hell? If 'all kinds of iniquities were performed by all, both singly and in common', we also share in the guilt of those not yet brought under the redemption wrought by Christ. Therefore we cannot rest on our oars until the last person on earth is also saved by the gospel of Christ. The heroes of faith enumerated in Hebrews 11 'did not receive what was promised, since God had foreseen something better for us, that apart from us they should not be made perfect' (verse 39f.). If so, apart from those not yet brought to the kingdom of Christ, we would not be made perfect. This, then is a part of the theology of a classless society.

C. H. Dodd's insight that there is a realized eschatology implied in the kingdom of God already inaugurated by Jesus Christ in history is an irrefutable one. We will not reach heaven beyond history if we do not experience it at least in part in history. The modern ecumenical movement, the new concern for social justice, the effort of the United Nations to bring the nations of the world together in peace and harmony, the organizations like UNCTAD seeking to develop the undeveloped nations etc., ought to take us further to the quick realization of the world government which should be the 'in common' aspect of the 'singly' aspect of the national governments. The world government is not to weaken the initiative of the national governments, but to help them to develop themselves at par with the developed nations. Wherever Christ begins to act and the Holy Spirit is allowed to work, an influx of love and new concern for the needy is irresistible. As Alexander Schmemann, the dean of St. Vladimir's Seminary in New York, has written, 'The phenomenon, inaccurately described as "primitive Christian communism" was not the product of any specifically christian economic or social theory, but a manifestation of love'.[32] Wherever there is self-giving love called agape, there is heaven, and wherever it is lacking, the cry for justice erupts into revolution, class war, and cut-throat competition leading to hell, the ultimate breach of human solidarity with God and with each other.

The final unity of individuality and collectivity would be around Jesus Christ the God-man in the fulness of the church or the kingdom of God and 'at the name of Jesus every knee should bow, in heaven and on earth, and under the earth and every tongue confess that Jesus Christ is Lord to the glory of God'.

7
THE SOCIETY AND THE INDIVIDUAL— IDENTITY AND DISTINCTION

The debate about the priority of the individual over society or of society over the individual is waning. The connection between the two is not more than that of the tree with the forest. There are isolated trees, but no isolated individuals. As Paul Tillich has rightly pointed out, personality is individualization by participation. The very birth or conception of the person is by the participation of the parents in the most intimate manner. Similarly a person can grow as a person only if love is poured into the person by others and by the society of the family, the neighbours, the church, the nation and even the world. It can be said in general that the individual owes to the society more than the society owes to the individual. Again, the family has a unity and identity in spite of the distinction between the father, the mother and the child. The very question as to who is prior does not arise at all in an ideal home.

The Holy Trinity is the Key

The relevance of the doctrine of the Trinity has never been greater than today. Many of the ideological debates of our period could be solved if only the doctrine of the Blessed Trinity were taken with the seriousness it deserves. The greatness of the patristic period was that the intellectual giants of that age like the Cappadocian Fathers saw how tremendous the significance of the Christian doctrine of the Trinity was and they spent their whole life defending and expounding it more than anything else. St. Basil's treatise on the Holy Spirit is a masterpiece even today and will remain so until the end of history. One of his main contentions in it is that sub-numeration is heretical and connumeration is the Christian way of equating the Father, the Son and the Holy Spirit in the Holy Trinity. Macedonius had applied the argument of the Arian subordination Christology to the Holy Spirit also and tried to establish that just as the Son is less than the Father, the Holy Spirit is less than the Son. The Cappadocian Fathers had the spiritual insight and the intellectual acumen to assert that there is co-equality, co-eternity and co-essentiality in the Blessed Trinity.

In the selfish, individualistic, capitalistic, competitive period which has conditioned our thinking we have uncon-sciously lost the solidarity of the family. Hence, even Karl Barth accused the Fathers of the eastern church of being guilty of tritheism. The easterners on the other hand accused Karl Barth of modalistic trinitarianism or Sabellianism. The east still has some possibility of having at least a faint peep into the unity in the eternal God-family of eternal Father, eternal Son and eternal Holy Spirit in the one triune God. The truth is that God is not a monad of exclusive monotheism nor a triad of tri-theism, but one eternal family where the Father, the Son and the Holy Spirit are equal and one in spite of the distinctions of fatherhood, motherhood and sonship.

Dinstinction does not nullify equality in the Holy Trinity. The Son is not the Father, but the Son is equal to the Father as a person. The mother is distinct from the father and the son, and yet if the family is a model one, the father and the mother would never argue the question as to who is superior. The chances are that each one would consider the other superior. In the image of the Trinity kept in the Satchidananda Ashram at Santhivanam near Trichinapoly, the shape of a woman is given for the Holy Spirit. Fr. Bede Griffith, the Superior of the Ashram, told me that the Holy Spirit is our Mother in the Godhead. Christians worship one God who is our Father, our Mother and our Brother, all in one person, a co-being being. Belonging to the women's liberation movement can be both healthy and unhealthy—healthy if it is to establish equality, but unhealthy if it is to nullify distinction. The equality of woman with man and of man with woman is as persons created in the image of God and not as persons for equal functions in the body of Christ.

The Blessed Virgin Mary has a status in all the ancient churches with that of the apostolic college, not as one of the twelve apostles, but as the mother of the church, symbolizing the totality of the church as she is the mother of the incarnate God. In order of priority in honour she comes before the apostles and the saints. She has a status which is in no way inferior to that of the apostles though she is not considered as a bishop or as an apostle. It is significant that it was an Orthodox lady delegate from the Soviet Union who argued at Nairobi that in the Orthodox Church women are not clamouring for ordination as in the Protestant churches since the women know that they have an equal status in the Church, as the blessed mother of God, though not specially ordained. I am not saying that this is to be taken as a theological argument against the ordination of women, but that the ultra-individualism of the Protestant theology without an adequate grasp of the doctrine of the Trinity is to be seen as one of the contributing factors for the argument that equality in status means equality in functions. The father who begets, the mother who gives birth and the son who is begotten are equal to one another and constitute an intimate sharing unity. Though the three are three individuals, they are one unity, one family, one centre, yes, even one person with one blood and one flesh. Rejoicing with those who rejoice and suffering with those who suffer is possible only in one family with deep solidarity in one blood.

The theological principle of *perichoresis* or co-inherence is a sound doctrine which teaches that where one person in the Trinity is at work the whole Trinity is involved. There is no water-tight distinction between the creator, the redeemer and the consummator as the one God is the creating Father, the redeeming Son and the perfecting Spirit. There is no more profound and at the same time no simpler truth than the doctrine of Trinity. 'Be ye therefore perfect even as your heavenly Father is perfect' is a commandment to be understood as trinitarian.

93

Wherein Lies Perfection?

Perfection is neither in the individual nor in the society, but in the sociality of the individual and the solidarity of the society. The heavenly Father's perfection itself is in his trinitarian existence. God who is a monad will be lacking in the actuality of love, possible only in a society, and tritheism will be lacking in the ontological unity that love, in perfection, experiences. The centrality of the fatherhood of God in the Christian revelation is the best symbol to express the nature and being of God as love. The perfection of love is always more deeply experienced in the best family. Our heavenly Father's perfection is in himself as he has the Son to love and to be loved and the Holy Spirit to share the love of the Father and the Son as the bond of love (*vinculum caritatis*). The perfection of his love is also in the trinitarian existence. In a happy family there is happiness in totality and in each of the three units. The mystery of Trinity is that the Son is perfect, the Holy Spirit is perfect, the Father is perfect just as the Trinity is perfect.

Selfishness is not only imperfection, but also sin. In an ideal family each lives for others and no one lives for himself. A mother does not enjoy eating food unless she shares it with her children. Sharing is a joy and not a burden in a family. Selfish accumulation of wealth is a sin in a society where others are in dire need. One who refuses to share is lacking in the Christian virtue of self-giving love. 'God so loved the world that he Gave.' A mother so loves her child that she gives. A neighbour so loves his neighbour that he gives. An employer so loves the employee that he gives. An employee so loves the employer that he gives his hard work for the project in which he is employed. Profit of one should be profit for all and loss of one should be loss for all.

The imperfection of the capitalistic system is the selfish motive of the employer or of the employee or of the total business concern without taking into consideration the plight of the teeming millions in the nation who are unemployed. There is no nation in the world where capitalism has solved the unemployment problem. Socialism of the right type has succeeded or can succeed in giving jobs to all the citizens of the country. The selfish profit motive of the capitalistic system is discernible in the artificial shortages created by false advertisement tricks, in the competitive manipulations of various companies and even in the agreement of producing companies to increase the price of a certain article to cheat the consumers. The view that has to be popularized is that there is no perfection in the part if there is no perfection in the whole. Therefore, the ideal to be aimed at is to work for one whole world family for 'poverty anywhere is a threat to prosperity everywhere'. Since it may take a long time to implement the international economic order for which all great thinkers of the world are raising their voices and for which even the one world government may be thrust on humanity by the forces of future circumstances, each nation must aim at teaching each citizen his duty for nation building.

The World a Nuclear Family

The new humanity God aims at is not a joint family of grandparents and cousins, but a nuclear family of God the Father, the church the mother, Jesus Christ the eldest brother and the whole humanity as direct brothers and sisters. All religions must evolve a theology of a classless society. Any hierarchical structure which cannot be accommodated to the Fatherhood of God leading to the brotherhood of man will be discarded in the world neighbourhood that is coming into being owing to the fast progress of world-wide communication systems and quick transportation facilities that science and technology have given us. The reality of sin and selfishness will continue to create havoc and thwart the plan of God, but all the narrow domestic walls of our time must be demolished and strenuous efforts made to bring about the world family. I know it is only a shallow optimist who would say that it is going to take place immediately. Yet, neither should we be entrenched pessimists who would laugh at any hopeful trend for the morrow. The very one world idea was a novelty in the time of the incarnate Lord who commissioned the church, 'Go ye unto all the world'. The spread of Christianity around the world was the first phenomenon in history to create a world-wide community. In our present century communism also has become a global reality. Other religions, parliamentary democracy, science and education are also bringing the world together. But we are bound to move faster in the future to a world-embracing human family.

Religions should not only avoid intolerance and be satisfied with tolerance or co-existence, but move on towards the love of all irrespective of caste, creed, colour or customs. When the Good Samaritan saw the wounded Jew, he did not ask him to become a Samaritan to receive the needed help. Any man in need is our neighbour, but only the man who shows mercy is behaving like a neighbour. Religion is to unite humanity and not to divide man from man. Conversion from one religion to another should certainly be allowed on the basis of faith or conviction, but not proselytism with the motive of gaining material benefits. Material benefits should be extended solely on the basis of need, irrespective of faith. As God gives rain to the just and the unjust since both are his children, we must help the good and the wicked, the rich and the poor, the religious and the irreligious, the theists and the atheists, for all are our brothers and sisters in creation.

The sin of the prodigal who stayed at home was that he could not accept that unacceptable prodigal brother as brother. It is significant that in the biblical parable of the prodigal sons, the prodigal who stayed at home is outside the home when the story ends and the prodigal who strayed away from home has entered the home with a penitential heart. Mutual acceptance is a precondition in the home. Jesus Christ the elder son did not stay at home when his younger brother was away from home, but went in search of him and brought him home. If we love only those who hold our views on all matters, we cannot even hope for a world family.

What about the elder prodigal who did not come inside when invited by the father? We must show the same attitude of the father to the disobedient. Did not the father say to him, 'My boy, you are always with me, and everything I have is yours. How could we help not celebrating this happy day? Your brother here was dead and has come back to life, was lost and is found?' Here again, the father holds him dear and near to him as the perfection of the family needs all in the family. If the elder prodigal did come in, he must have come in with a new

96

heart and a new attitude to his brother. If he did not come in, the gate remains open for him to come at any time he repents. Similarly, the world family of God has an inner circle of those who accept the Father and each other and an outer circle who are accepted by the Father but who do not accept the Father. God does not use totalitarian means to bring in any one as he himself has shared his own freedom with his children and does not want to treat them as slaves.

The Omega Point

When Jesus Christ says, 'I am Alpha and Omega', it is an eternal 'I AM'. He is Jehovah, I AM THAT I AM, in history and in eternity. It is noteworthy that this claim of the Lord is recorded in the first and last chapters and the penultimate chapter of Revelation (1:8; 22:13; 21:6). He is the uniting point of creation and consummation, of history and eternity, of beginning and end of all things visible and invisible. Teilhard de Chardin relates the whole process of evolution to Jesus Christ, the alpha point and the omega point. The cosmic Christology of St. Paul (e.g. Col.1:15–20) asserts that the whole universe has been created 'through him and for him'. Any narrow view of Christ which claims him only as the head of the baptized community ignores both the logos and the cosmic Christologies. 'For in him, the complete being of God, by God's own choice, came to dwell. Through him God chose to reconcile the whole universe to himself, making peace through the shedding of the blood upon the cross to reconcile all things, whether on earth or in heaven, through him alone' (Col.1:19f.).

Many theologians of today find the presence of Christ in other religions as *logoi spermatikoi* (scattered seeds of truth), the unknown Christ of Hinduism (Raymond Panikkar), the logos (reason) that was in the world from the time of creation by Christ the eternal logos and as the omnipresent God who is identical with the incarnate God, Jesus Christ. The Nairobi Report of Section III dealing with the World Community and Living Faiths points out that 'Jesus Christ restores what is truly human in any culture and frees us to be open to other cultures' (page 5). Section IV on Education for Liberation and Community adds, 'Christ gives us the vision and the promise of a new world, the basis for its renewal and the power to realize it, both in our personal life and in the life of the community' (page 1). Section I on Confessing Christ Today has boldly presented a wholistic approach calling the church to present the whole gospel for the whole person and the whole world.

Jesus Christ is the same yesterday, today and for ever. Yet he has an existential manifestation of his perfection in its omega point, which would be richer than that of the alpha point. The perfection of the alpha point is that of the bud while that of the omega point is that of the flower in full bloom. The tri-unity is hidden in the alpha point and every point in God's eternity. Jesus Christ does not exist as a distinct person alone in the Godhead, but also with perfect identity. The Father and the Holy Spirit are in Christ just as Christ is in the Godhead together with the Holy Spirit. Every point in the Trinity is a tri-point i.e. there is no exclusive singularity in the Godhead nor in Christian existence. The alpha point is a tri-point and the omega point will be a richer tri-point due to the continuing work of the Holy Spirit in the church and the world.

Now Darkly then Face to Face

'Now we see in a mirror dimly, but then face to face.' The unity of plurality and the plurality of unity are not yet fully seen or manifested in the church, the nation or the world. The Hegelian dialectic of ideas or spirit and the Marxian dialectic of materialism are also seeing the perfection only through a mirror dimly. Even the individualism of the Roman Catholic papacy and of Protestant freedom of the individual on the one hand, and of Orthodox *sobornost* or universality will meet together in the one ecumenical church of the future. The dignity of the individual person and the togetherness of socialism will also find a meeting point in the social justice of the kingdom of God or world family towards which human-ity will be slowly moving in the future. The world 'collegial-ity' to which the Second Vatican Council called the attention of the church has a richness which has to be discovered today or tomorrow.

True democracy is not irreconcilable with the true hierarchical structure of the church based on the model of the Holy Trinity. Collegial hierarchy is the precaution against democracy degenerating into congregationalism and hierarchy degenerating into autocratic despotism. Collegiality must be applied from top to bottom and from bottom to top. The motto of all ecumenical councils is given by the very first ecumenical council of Jerusalem, 'It has seemed good to the Holy Spirit and to us'. When the Holy Spirit is at work, unanimity is not an impossibility. The Roman Catholic Church of yesterday taught that error had no right to exist and persecuted the non-Roman Churches in Spain and South America. The Roman Catholic Church of today is giving importance to religious freedom, thanks to the spirit of God that worked through Pope John who called the council and opened the window for fresh air into the church. The Roman Catholic Church of tomorrow must be ready to apply the principle of trinitarian collegiality to papacy also and discover the profundity of the venerable old tradition of *primus inter pares*.

My thesis in this chapter is that the whole truth is always trinitarian and not binitarian or unitarian. This is to be manifested in the unity of father, mother and child, unity of parliament, judiciary and executive, unity of unconscious, pre-conscious and conscious mind, as the unity of the Father, the Son and the Holy Spirit in one Godhead.

8
WE AND THE POOR

'There will never be any poor among you if only you will obey the Lord' (Deut. 15:4).

This verse is seldom quoted. But 'the poor will never cease out of the land' (verse 11) is often quoted. We know that 'poverty anywhere is a threat to prosperity everywhere'. The plan of God is certainly to 'put down the mighty from their thrones and exalt those of a low degree' (Luke 1:52). These two processes march on hand in hand. The progress of creating an egalitarian society has been faster in the socialist countries and slower in others. The Christian churches around the world have always extended a sympathetic hand towards the poor, but have not struck at the root of the penury. Hence, a self-examination to discover our own sins, a penitential heart if found guilty, and a new life style are indispensable if we are to escape the wrath of God.

The Cause of Poverty

'There was not a needy person among them' (Acts 4:34) when they were filled by the Holy Spirit and shared everything personal for the use of all in the fellowship. Pentecost was a reconciliation towards God and fellow men in an intimate manner. 'No one said that any of the things which he possessed was his own, but they had everything in common' (2:32). This is inevitable when the Holy Spirit becomes the one active agent among many people. Ultra-individualism started when Cain felt rejected by God and consequently hated his own brother. The solidarity of the family of Adam was lost by the fall. The fall itself took place when the authority of God over the whole garden was challenged by Adam, instigated by satan. 'The Lord God took the man and put him in the garden of Eden to till it and to keep it' (Gen. 2:15). But Adam felt it his right to pluck the fruit of the forbidden tree and went beyond the bounds of stewardship. Ananias and Sapphira also lost the sense of stewardship and fell by hiding a part of the proceeds of the sale of their God-given land for their own use. The joy of *koinonia* and the experience of Pentecost was lost when selfishness crept in. The false expectation of the imminent return of the Lord also led to the creation of 'have's' and 'have not's'.

Thus the twofold alienations, vertically from God and horizontally from the neighbour, are two aspects of one fall. Adam did not obey the commandment of the Lord 'to till it and to keep it' and not to own it. He felt he owned the garden. The demand for private property without a sense of steward-ship is both the cause and effect of the fall. Adam should have felt that 'the whole world and the fullness thereof belongs to God (Psa. 24:1). Ananias should have felt that the property sold was his own by the grace of God and not by any inherent right over property. David knew that the whole wealth of the whole world was God's. 'Both riches and honour come from thee . . . For all things come from thee, and of thy own have we given thee' (1 Chron. 29:10–14).

What then is the cause of poverty? It is the selfishness of man or the fall of man. The guilt of selfishness is universal, but the expression of it is greater wherever individual freedom is exalted over social justice. The checks suggested by God to curtail the selfish accumulation of wealth by the observance of every 7th year as the Year of Release when 'every creditor shall release what he has lent to his neighbour' (Deut. 15:2) and the 50th year as the Year of Jubilee when an equalization process of wealth would take place (Lev. 25) were not implemented by the Jews because of their sinfulness. Similarly, we do not obey the two greatest commandments and so poverty is rampant not only in the Third World, but everywhere.

The Universality of Poverty

Poverty is not only material but also mental and spiritual. A rich man is spiritually poor and so our Lord wanted the rich young ruler to sell everything he had and give it to the poor so that he might become spiritually rich and worthy to follow the self-emptied Saviour of the world (Mark 10:17–22). In the parable of the great banquet that our Lord told, all those who had private property could not enjoy the banquet of the kingdom of God, but 'the poor, the maimed, the blind and the lame' could. Here the materially rich are spiritually poor and the materially poor are spiritually rich (Luke 14:15–24). Our Lord considered the poor widow who put only two copper coins in the treasury richer than those who 'contributed out of their abundance' (Mark 12:41–44). The change that took place in the heart of Zacchaeus at our Lord's visit to his home was so revolutionary that he became materially poor due to the spiritual riches he received and uttered in ecstatic joy, 'Behold Lord, half of my goods I give to the poor; and if I have defrauded anyone of anything, I restore it fourfold' (Luke 19:8). It was a public manifestation of the fact that salvation had come to his heart and home and he became truly rich in the sight of God. In the parable of the rich man and Lazarus, the spiritual poverty of the rich man was that he allowed his neighbour to be poor when he himself was rich (Luke 16:19–31). Hence, in the new kingdom Lazarus is truly rich and the rich man is in need and poverty.

The universality of poverty is due to the universality of sin. Poverty is lack of something very essential for life. God alone is rich in the sense that he lacks nothing. Are there human beings in the world who lack nothing? Our Lord told the young rich ruler who thought that he lacked nothing, 'You lack one thing'. What was it that he lacked? He lacked concern about his neighbour and accumulated wealth for himself. It was by self-deception that he said he had observed all the commandments from his youth. If he had loved his neighbour as he loved himself, he would not have become rich. How can anyone become rich in a poor world and claim that he loves his neighbour as himself? Anyone who is rich has become rich by his poverty of self-giving Christian love. Real Christian love is capable of creating a classless society.

In the parable of the Good Samaritan, the question asked was 'Who is my neighbour?' and the question asked by our Lord to the questioner at the end of the parable was 'Which of

103

these do you think proved neighbour to the man who fell among the robbers?' (Luke 10:29–37). The questioner gives the answer, 'The one who showed mercy on him'. The robbers stand for the world which does not show mercy, but goes on robbing and exploiting by black-marketing or any other means whereby the neighbour is made poor. The priest and the Levite stand for the modern merciless Christians and religious persons who ignore the appalling need of the world and pass by on the other side to worship in the church, temple or mosque. The only one who showed mercy was the Good Samaritan who stands for the crucified and risen Christ. Except for him all are sinners. The extremely poor are often living like animals and the extremely rich are callous like beasts in any society where there are two irreconcilable classes of people, namely the poor and the rich.

The Rich Must Become Poor Voluntarily

There is no easy solution for economic inequalities in a finite world. It is utopian to expect 4 billion billionnaires in our world. The selfish ambition of any one to become a millionaire in a world of poverty and hunger is to be checked by one's own conscience saturated by Christian teaching. On the other hand, the rich must be taught the joy of following the master's example, 'For you know how generous our Lord Jesus Christ has been; he was rich, yet for your sake he became poor, so that through his poverty you might become rich' (2 Cor. 8:9). The richest Son of God became the poorest son of man in the person of Jesus Christ, the Saviour of the world. He is not only the redeemer of the world, but also the model. Hence we have to take up the cross and follow him. We cannot categorize Jesus Christ with the rich or with the poor as man-in-God and God-in-man and yet when God became man, it was with the poor that he identified himself. His voluntary self-emptying (*kenosis*) (Phil. 2:5–11) is the pattern for the church and the Christian to emulate.

A simpler life style is indispensable to avoid the dangers of the unscrupulous use of the natural resources and because of the kenotic nature of Christian love. As my Indonesian friend

104

Soritua Naban reminded church leaders, 'We have to ask in all humility what we have done to develop a simpler life style both within our own circle and in the wider society. Our failure to live up to this calling betrays our lack of understanding of what the shalom of Christ demands of us'.[33] Metropolitan Paulos Gregorios pointed out in Sydney in July 1976, 'What the world is looking for is a community which shows it how to live, a pattern, a design in which human beings can live in relation to each other, and produce and distribute and consume in such a way that both humanity and the rest of the creation can flourish'.[34] Are they not also pleading for a classless society?

Bishop Mortiner Arias was right at Nairobi in comparing the gospel with manna, it cannot be kept. 'If we do not share it, we lose it. If we do not use it, it goes stale.' May I add that wealth is also like manna. If we do not share it, we lose it. Sharing is not a burden but a joyful affair in Christian life. 'God so loved the world that he gave . . .' Love is that in which the lover shares gladly everything with the loved. Parents who work hard and share happily the results of their hard work with their children tell us that sharing is an ecstatic experience. One verse which our Lord uttered but which the gospels did not record has come down to us from St. Paul's Miletus address to the Ephesian elders, 'Happiness lies more in giving than in receiving' (Acts 20:35).

Psychologists point out that introverted persons are unhappy because selfishness hardens the heart and takes the joy out of your heart. Thus, the perfect love of God and the love of neighbour as yourself are the best ways of overcoming the unhappiness of an introverted life. In fact, these two vertical and horizontal dimensions of life with a Christoverted centre is the very essence of Christianity. We are not asked to love the neighbour as a neighbour, but as ourselves. The poor neighbour is myself and I am asked to love him as I love myself. This is impossible if we do not have the mind of Christ. Christ Jesus had nothing for himself that he did not share with others joyfully. Even his death was for the whole of humanity. He died and rose again for the whole of humanity.

What Does the Poor Neighbour Need?

My friend C. I. Itty was right in telling the 4th UNCTAD Conference at Nairobi in May 1976 that, 'The struggle of the poor and the oppressed is not merely for food and other necessities, but also for freedom, dignity, creativity, and participation in the decision-making that effects their lives. Because poverty has its roots in unjust systems and structures that oblige the poor to subsidize the rich, the development process inevitably involves efforts aimed at systemic changes on local, national and international levels'.

The poor are interested in eradicating poverty everywhere and in creating an international economic order based on human solidarity as well as making available the resources of the whole world for all its inhabitants wherever they are.

Though many would consider a world government as a utopian dream, the days are fast approaching when co-existence will be difficult without corporate existence, and social justice on a world level will be impossible without a world government.

The goal of a classless society is a potent weapon Karl Marx borrowed from the Christian premises and mixed it up with the questionable doctrine of the inevitability of class war. The poor of the world are interested in a theology of a classless society about which the theologians of the world are afraid to speak lest they be mistaken to be communists.

The right to work is more basic than the right to accumulate private property and huge bank-balances. It is a well known fact of history that only the countries which practise socialism have solved the problem of unemployment. The command of St. Paul, 'The man who will not work shall not eat' (2 Thes. 3:10) has to be disobeyed by the teeming millions of unemployed people in all countries where capitalism and mixed economy are practised. The opportunity to work and live is the birth-right of all people who are healthy, but the right to private property is causing unjust exploitation of the majority by the minority. As Itty added at UNCTAD, 'When 30% of the world's population owns nearly three-quarters of the world's resources, maldistribution is inevitable'.

The need of the poor is the need of the rich as 'God has made of one blood all nations of men to dwell on all the face of the earth'. The increasing gap between the rich and the poor has to be bridged as quickly as possible locally, nationally and internationally. There is no hope for the poor if the rich continue to control the world market and hold on to the present luxuries of life and keep their technological know-how to themselves. We should not ask the old question of Cain, 'Am I my brother's keeper?' Our Lord's answer is 'You are not your brother's keeper, but your brother's *brother*'.

9
THE SERMON ON THE MOUNT—
ETHICS OF A CLASSLESS SOCIETY

Reinhold Niebuhr considers the Sermon on the Mount as an 'impossible possibility'. He is right in asserting that it is not an easy possibility for life on earth and it is not the ethics of the secular state. Mahatma Gandhi and Leo Tolstoy take it as a blue-print for life here and now. They would, however, agree that it is not being practised in our class-structured society. Vincent Taylor and others would take it as the standard in the kingdom of God before which we would be driven to penitence and would want to confess our sins before God. It is my considered opinion that it is not eschatological ethics to be practised in the world to come, as no one there is likely to beat on our right cheek or sue and take our coat. The impossibility of obeying the Sermon on the Mount is greater in the valley than on the mountain-top with the Lord. Wherever the triune God is present, and his presence is felt by the people, there is a classless society and on that mountain, it is easier to practise its ethical teachings.

The first part of the Sermon (Matt. 5:3–16), which includes the beatitudes, is asking for a simple life style of poverty, repentance, meekness, justice, mercy, purity of heart, peace-making and the readiness to suffer for righteousness' sake, which are all ethical standards of a classless society. We know that the Lukan version of the beatitudes is in the second person and does not contain 'in spirit' when speaking of the poverty: 'Blessed are you poor, for yours is the kingdom of God. Blessed are you who hunger now, for you shall be satisfied . . .' (Luke 6:20–22). Furthermore, 4 'woe to you' passages are added there and each of them is against those who belong to the top class of a class-ridden society, 'Woe to you that are rich, for you have received your consolation. Woe to you that are full now, for you shall hunger. Woe to you that laugh now, for you shall mourn and weep. Woe to you, when all men speak well of you, for so their fathers did to the false prophets' (6:24–26).

The question of the Christian conscience is 'Why should I be rich when my neighbour is poor?' Poverty is of two kinds, that which society or others impose on us and that which we accept voluntarily. The poverty of the kingdom of God is that which its citizens accept voluntarily and gladly. They are like the salt that has not lost its taste, but has lost itself to give taste to other things, and the light of the world which burns itself to give light to others. It is significant that each saint is salt for the whole earth and light for the whole world. This is the ethic of one world and not a parochial or national ethic of self-interest of the class-ridden society. 'Let your light so shine before men (not just before your own house or class) that they may see your good works and give glory to your Father (who is also the Father of the whole of humanity) who is in heaven.' Those who revile and persecute the saints of God are also their kith and kin and brothers who have become prodigals and so we have to pray for them also.

The second part of the Sermon (Matt. 5:17–48) which has 'but I say unto you' repeated 6 times, is a clear picture of the contrasts between the class-ridden society and the new society.

Class-structured society of law	*Classless society of the Gospel*
1. Do not kill.	Do not be angry. Be reconciled to your brother. Make friends quickly with your accuser.
2. Do not commit adultery.	Do not look at a woman lustfully because she is your spiritual sister belonging to your own family.
3. Divorce with certificate of divorce.	No divorce except on the ground of unchastity (cf. Mark 10:11–12).

110

4. Do not swear falsely.	Do not swear at all. How can you lie to a member of your own family?
5. Love neighbour, hate enemy.	Love your enemies. They also belong to your own family and are your brothers and sisters.
6. An eye for an eye and a tooth for a tooth.	Give to him who begs from you, and do not refuse him who would borrow from you. (Treat all as members of your own family.)

It is very clear from the above summary of the second section of the Sermon that unless we consider all as members of our own family we will not be able to obey these commandments.

The third section (Matt. 6:1–18) is about the Godward, manward and inward relations of a citizen of the classless society. The key idea behind all three is its secrecy. In our class-structured society, hardly anything is done without advertisement, publicity and propaganda. The hypocrites of old used to sound trumpets in the market place to attract poor people to them and give them alms to earn name and fame. Similarly, if we build a house for a poor man, we want to publish pictures of the house, the giver and the recipient and we humiliate him. But we do not make any such publicity when we build houses for our own children. The command of our Lord, 'When you give alms, do not let your left hand know what your right hand is doing' is not at all heeded in the capitalistic societies of the world.

The prayer 'Our Father who art in heaven' is the model prayer of a classless society. The first person singular does not appear anywhere in it. After praying for the glory of God's name, kingdom and will, all the 4 petitions are for the whole society of the whole world and not for the single Christian. 'Give us this day our daily bread' is a prayer for provisions for all the people of the whole earth for each day and not for daily or yearly cake for any particular person. In fact it means, 'Lord give me no more than the share of one person having divided the bread of the whole world for all the people of the world'. Pardon too is for all people in the petition, 'forgive us our debts as we have forgiven our debtors'. The one and only condition in the whole prayer is that divine pardon is based on the pardoning heart of the petitioner. If anyone has hatred against anyone else, he is not supposed to pray this prayer hypocritically. In a classless society there should be no enemies. Preservation from temptation and protection from the evil one is also requested for all people and not just for the individual who prays. The invocation 'Our Father . . .' shows our solidarity with all our fellowmen who are our brothers and sisters. It is not a prayer addressed to 'Our Grandfather in heaven' because then there would be first cousins and second cousins among us. But we are all members of one nuclear family and so one classless society.

Fasting is a way of self discipline. It is to be done joyfully and not as imposed from above. 'When you fast, anoint your head and wash your face, that your fasting may not be seen by men.' In a classless society, nothing is to be achieved in being seen by men as all are one family. 'Your Father who sees in secret will reward you.' Everything, good deeds, prayer and fasting, which include the three-fold life of each Christian is for the whole community, even when done in secret. In a classless society, no one is over anxious about his personal needs. It is the spiritual and material needs of the whole community that matter.

The fourth section (Matt. 6:19–7:27) contains 10 commandments which go beyond the decalogue (Ex. 20:2–17). They can be obeyed only in a proletarian, classless society. The state would make it easy for us to obey them. Our Lord must have envisaged the world of tomorrow with too many mouths to feed and too little resources available to give such commandments for frugality. It is not only those in the developed countries who have laid up treasures on earth. The upper class people of all countries must read the Sermon afresh and realize that they are going diametrically opposite to it. The World Council of Churches studying the theme 'Sustainable Society' should come forward with a definite stand for a

112

classless society. Let us peruse these commandments and see how they fit in in the new society.

1. 'Do not lay up for yourselves treasures on earth . . . but lay up for yourselves treasures in heaven . . . For where your treasure is, there will your heart be also.' Our interest has to shift from money to men, from earthly possessions to lasting achievements. In our class structure, the top-most class has plenty of money in the bank and the lowest class has nothing even in the stomach. The last part of this command, when reworded would mean, 'Where your heart is, there your treasure also will be'. As our hearts are in our own comforts and in the bright future of our children, we lay up treasures for ourselves and our offspring. When our hearts are set on God and on all his children, our treasure will also be spent for them as gladly as we keep it for ourselves. This first commandment is of paramount importance and it is better to take it seriously and work for the welfare of all than be selfish.

2. 'If then the light in you is darkness, how great is the darkness.' The second commandment is to open our spiritual eyes and see the plight of the lost, the least and the last of whom we do not take any notice in our social existence. When the richest meet they have dialogue with their own class, the middle with the middle and the lowest with the lowest. Is not the Rotary Club just for a class of people into whom the lowest class is never invited though some charity may be extended to them? Their motto 'service above self' must change into 'selfless service'. A classless society would open its eyes and see man as man, brother as brother and not as categorized by their money or degrees or family status or dress. Our spiritual eyes need treatment.

3. 'You cannot serve two masters.' Most of us are serving God and mammon (which means profit). The four attempts that are being tried now are (a) forsaking God and serving money, (b) serving God and money, (c) forsaking money and serving God, and (d) using money for the service of God and fellowmen. It is the last of these that is advocated in a classless society. When wealth becomes a tool to help fellowmen and not an end in itself, we find a new joy which money cannot give.

4. 'Do not be anxious about your life . . . drink . . . food . . .

clothing.' Anxiety has become a neurosis in developed countries. Someone joked, 'An average American believes in three things, life, liberty and a new car in pursuit of happiness'. The craze for a more luxurious life, costly drinks, new fashions in clothing and expensive food has become a sickness of the rich in every society. Our Lord's statement to the Samaritan woman remains unchallenged to this day, 'Everyone who drinks of this water will thirst again'. The cure for the increasing anxiety, mental diseases, frustration and despair of our modern culture is a simpler life style for all. How sinful we are when we are anxious about the morrow of our own lives without a little anxiety about the today of our neighbours. But in a classless society where everyone works hard for all and all are deeply concerned about the welfare of each this commandment is also easy to be obeyed. The sense of security of each earned by each has a hidden insecurity in an insecure world. The only remedy is to bring about a security for all by the labours of all. This commandment is concluded with the classic statement, 'Seek first his kingdom and his righteousness, and all these things shall be yours as well'. Is not the classless society a better kingdom of God than the world of ours without a solidarity?

5. 'Judge not that you be not judged.' We judge others when we do not consider them as our brothers and say 'let me take the speck out of your eye'. We have a real interest in finding fault with those who are not on good terms with us. Hardly anyone would want to expose the mistake of their loved ones to those outside. Many litigations will also end when a classless society is really infected with mutual love and concern.

6. 'Do not throw your pearls before swine.' We are asked not to mix the sublime with the ridiculous. No human being is to be regarded as a dog or a pig. Our fellowmen are all holy pearls and they should not be despised.

7. 'Ask and it will be given you, seek and you will find; knock, and it will be opened to you . . .' We cannot bring about a classless society by our own efforts. It is God who is ruling and over-ruling in the affairs of man. All our efforts have to be prayerful. Asking God for a new world, seeking his ways to achieve it and knocking at his door for provisions are

114

all sacred responsibilities committed to us by the Lord. Furthermore, we can be optimistic since God is better than our human parents and even they will not give us anything harmful. The golden rule comes at the conclusion of this commandment, 'So whatever you wish that men would do to you, do so to them; for this is the law and the prophets'. It is only in a classless society that we can do to others as we would like others do to us. As there is a solidarity with all, this is a possibility.

8. 'Enter by the narrow gate . . .' The classless society will not be an easy achievement. It is only very few of my readers who would be ready for the theology of a classless society. But we are now going through a broad way leading to destruction. This is what the scientists also are reminding us.

9. 'Beware of false prophets . . .' They tell us that we are on the right track. They tell us that we cannot set the clock back and that in spite of *Future Shock,* we can have a better standard of life for billions of people on earth.

10. 'Not every one who says to me, "Lord, Lord" shall enter the kingdom of heaven, but he who does the will of God.' Here is the crux of the whole matter. All the talk about the classless society will not cut any ice unless and until we work for it with our whole heart and mind and soul. As the conclusion of the Sermon says the house built on the rock of love and justice alone will stand and that built on selfishness will fall and future historians will say, 'Great was the fall of it.'

10
A CLASSLESS SOCIETY—BUT HOW?

A classless society is the ideal. It is the meaning of Christian sharing fellowship or *koinonia*. The church is a *koinonia* within which there is no discrimination between the Jew and the Gentile, the Greek, Barbarian and Scythian, male and female. All are one in Christ. St. Paul wanted the rich Philemon to accept the slave Onesimus as a brother. The church is a brotherhood working for a world brotherhood. None is allowed to be selfish in the church because all are to have the mind of Christ and Christ was never selfish. Christian love and selfishness cannot go together. Any theology worth its name has to be the theology of a classless society. Theology, being the science of God, has to be God-centred. If God is the centre, the driving force and the eternal logos, everything related to him has to be like him and he is the perfect classless society of one in three and three in one, the eternal unity of family, the perfect co-being, the ontological perfection of love in eternal action.

Therefore, any valid theology which accepts the Holy Trinity as basic and decisive has to be a theology of a classless society, whether it is Orthodox or Roman Catholic or Protestant. A class-structured society is not a perfect unity and so has to be discarded as less than the ideal. All animosities between employer and employee, master and servant, ruler and ruled, neighbour and neighbour are the outcome of sin and selfishness and there is no theology which can justify these opposites as God-ordered. The Christian theology of *koinonia* has to be explained as a theology of a classless society to our class-oriented world of the rich and the poor in perpetual conflict. If the reader agrees that Christian theology is to pave the way for the kingdom of God or the family of God, it is then expected that he will work for a classless society of equality, fraternity and freedom.

I must then try to answer the natural question raised by well-meaning readers who say, 'Yes, a classless society is the ideal, but how to arrive at one? Is it possible in this fallen world? Should we not wait for the second coming of our Lord for such a perfection?'

Realize that it is Utopian and yet not Utopian

What do we mean when we pray daily, 'Thy Kingdom come *on earth* as it is in heaven'? Heaven on earth is perfection on earth which is utopian and still we pray daily for it knowing that with God all things are possible. The realization of perfection in history is being delayed and thwarted by our sinfulness, selfishness, pride and despair, yet we know that Christ is the answer both today and tomorrow. His return to earth at the consummation of history is one of the articles of the Nicene Creed and it is squarely based on the biblical witness. Whether he comes again when things are at their worst as some theologians hold, or whether there will be progress in history since there is a realized eschatology from the time of his first coming as the majority of theologians hold, we have to pray and work for his coming *on earth*.

The former view does not take the effect of the incarnation seriously, nor the work of the Holy Spirit in the church and the world seriously. An objective study of history from the time of the incarnation until today is against any shallow optimism, and against utter pessimism. Certainly there will be wicked people in history until its end, but the Holy Spirit is convincing the world of sin, righteousness and judgement in an increasing measure with the passing of time. The very subject of social justice is more seriously studied today than ever before. This is not done in the church alone, but also outside and the Holy Spirit is behind both.

Our Lord taught his disciples another lesson which is also utopian, 'Be ye therefore perfect as your heavenly Father is perfect'. The point is that perfection must be aimed at whether we attain the same in history or beyond history, progressively or antithetically. We shall never reach Mount Everest if we do not make it our goal. The Everest of heaven is unattainable in

118

history and yet we can die happily if we are assured that we die climbing towards the goal and that the climbing can be continued even after the grave. Hinduism teaches that there are *jivanmuktas* who attain perfection while remaining in body and also *videha-muktas* who attain liberation only after death. According to the Christian faith, only Jesus Christ has walked the face of the earth perfect and sinless and that was due to his uniqueness as the only incarnation of the word in the world. Christian saints are not those who had no consciousness of sin as Jesus Christ. Many of the saints regarded themselves as the greatest sinners, though their faults were microscopic in the sight of others. We are the ones who consider them as saints and none of them claimed any unique status for themselves. The perfection of a classless society is an impossible possibility and yet we must aim at it and work for it as long as we are taught to pray, and continue to pray, 'Thy kingdom come on earth'.

'The Pedagogy of the Oppressed'

The new educational system recommended by Paulo Freire in his famous book *The Pedagogy of the Oppressed*[35] and other writings[36] must be studied critically by us in India since the situation here is very different from that in Brazil and other countries of South America regarding class structure and the exploitation of one class by another. The writings of Archbishop Helder Camera[37] are also worth studying. His aim is education for the creation of a classless society. Our present education system has been evolved by the rich class down the centuries from the time of the Greek philosophers and it will perpetuate the present two story humanity consisting of the teacher and the taught, the rich and the poor, the employer and the employee, the oppresser and the oppressed, the exploiter and the exploited, those who wield power and the powerless, ruler and ruled, those who know the sense of human worth and dignity and those who have no consciousness of their own dignity, those who control the media of communications and those who are manipulated by such class propaganda, the person and the 'object being', the

119

speaking few and the listening many, the makers of history and the silent, uncritical victims of historical forces that control them, those who can help others and yet do not help the helpless majority.

The tragedy of such a system is that neither of these classes is liberated from selfishness and apathy. The upper class thinks that it knows but does not know that it is chained by selfishness, and the lower class is utterly ignorant of the simple fact that the rich are all rich because of the poverty of the poor. Our present educational style which Paulo Freire rightly calls 'Banking System' is not a dialogue method or a free discussion method. The ideas that the teachers deposit in the minds of the students are those which they inherited from their own class which saw to it that their own interests were kept unaffected. This value system is not creating a new value for a classless humanity but only spreading the existing values of a class society. The 'closed stratification' of the existing pedagogy has already divided humanity into many classes—the Brahmins, the Kahatriyas, the Vaisyas, the Sudras, the Harijans in India. The existing teaching methods are helpful to 'domesticate' the exploited, uncritical, inferior, powerless majority to remain in their pathetic condition.

The pedagogy of the oppressed, on the other hand, is to raise the dignity, consciousness, critical sense and the challenge of the mass of people at the lowest strata of our society and to humanise them. Any liberation anywhere has taken place only through a pedagogy of the oppressed, whether it was of India from the British yoke, or of China from the grip of Chiang Kai-shek or of the colonial people of Africa from the foreign rulers. Similarly, the poor people of the world must be liberated themselves from their own indifference and apathy if they are to be liberated from the exploiting rich class in their own midst or outside their countries.

Many of the oppressed do not know the acuteness of the oppression of the rich. Just as the majority of Indians before and at the time of Mahatma Gandhi were not conscious of the exploitation of the British government and merchants in India because of the railways they built, the English education they brought and many other fringe benefits, the majority of the oppressed people of the world are not conscious of the simple fact that they work and the rich get the benefits in a large measure. Do the millions who pluck tea in the teagardens of the rich estate owners and live in miserable conditions realize that profit of the estate has been disproportionately used by the owner for his huge bungalow, expensive car, luxurious life style, and that he has got black and white money in his custody—all because many poor people work for him for a pittance? Therefore conscientization of the oppressed is highly necessary and education must have it as the main objective.

This will not be done by the rich and the oppressor because they are naturally conditioned by self-interest and they are capable of torpedoing this in as many ways as possible. Hence the poor themselves must take the initiative for the education of the poor in such a way that they can tell the rich boldly that they are robbers who have robbed the result of their sweat and blood and have converted it into an unjustifiable life style and luxury goods when they themselves are far below the poverty line. There may be a few among the rich who are also humanised and they may join with the poor to create a classless society and they must be welcomed by the poor majority.

The Pedagogy for the Oppressor

One of the most unfortunate naked truths of our time is that many of the oppressors do not realize that they control the means of production to suit their profit motive, the mass media to spread falsehood and the curriculum to continue the present exploitative system. Some of the greatest hymns of the Christian hymnals have been written by slave trading Christian planters in the ships that were bringing slaves in chains from Africa to work in their plantations in America. They may not have seen any crime in slave traffic in those days for they had an innocent conscience attuned to their own self-interest and callous to the suffering of others. We are not entirely free from the conditioning forces of our capitalistic and class oriented educational system. Therefore we are also practising slave traffic in a different garb, not recognizing that

121

we are exploiters and sinners. The slave traders of the 18th century must have justified their action on the grounds that they paid cash to purchase the slaves who would otherwise have died of starvation. Similarly the rich contractors, employers, estate owners and other proprietors of private enterprises think that they are doing a great service to their country and the poor by providing jobs and solving the intolerable problem of unemployment. The fact, however, is that no capitalistic country of our world has solved unemployment. Socialistic countries alone have succeeded in giving jobs to all their citizens. The question whether it is possible to evolve a responsible society with the individual initiative which capitalism stresses and the social justice which socialism wants, is not yet answered satisfactorily even in Israel where an attempt is being made.

It is easy to prepare a syllabus for the pedagogy of the oppressor if we take the Christian revelation seriously. Christian theology, pure and simple, is sufficient for it (see chapter IV). The Christian doctrine of God is that there is no inequality in the Holy Trinity in spite of the eternal distinctions. The Christian doctrine of man is that 'God has made of one blood all nations of men to dwell on all the face of the earth' and that there is the same image of God in every man. All the inequalities between brother and brother that took place because of the fall have been undone by the richest son of God who became the poorest son of man and created an egalitarian church at Pentecost by the work of the Holy Spirit. The identification of the incarnate Lord with the poor and the oppressed of the world has set the model for an incarnational and kenotic mission of the church. The world, according to scripture, is the creation of God and still belongs to God and does not belong to any man as his private property. Adam was put in the garden of Eden to 'till it and to keep it' and not to own it. It was also to assert the ownership of God that Adam was forbidden to eat from 'the tree in the midst of the garden'. Satan beguiled Adam and Eve and they ate from the forbidden tree as if they were the owners of the garden. The Christian teaching on stewardship is to be taught to the rich to remove the fallacy in their minds that they own the land or the means of production or money or time or talents. All these are the gifts of God to be used for the family of God including all his children.

The Christian ethic of love must be taught in such a way that it includes social justice. There is the Christless love of Zacchaeus which had taught him to give half his goods to the poor out of a false sense that that would atone for the cheating he used to practise in tax collection. What Zacchaeus told our Lord can also mean 'Lord, I am in the habit of giving half of my goods to the poor, but now that you have come into my home and life, if I have defrauded anyone or anything, I restore it fourfold'. The rich should not be satisfied with charity, but must practise justice. Social justice demands that all the food, clothing, shelter, medicine and work are to be shared by all the people of the whole world, because they belong to the common Father of us all and are meant for all his children and not for a few. Love without justice is mere emotion, justice without love is dead law, but love with justice is Christian. What happened to Zacchaeus was a terrific conscientization that ought to happen in the presence of Jesus Christ to any oppressor.

The pedagogy of the oppressor is to convince him or her that in a class-structured society both the classes are in sin. The superior class is guilty of the sin of a superiority complex and the inferior class of an inferiority complex. The rich get sick by over-eating and the poor get sick by under-eating. The rich lady with many costly sarees worries as to which one to wear for a pompous party and the poor girl with only one cheap and torn saree worries as to whom to borrow a saree from for a friend's wedding party. The rich old lady left alone in a palatial building by her only son who is abroad cannot get enough servants to keep the house clean and wants to live in a smaller house, and the parents of many children sleeping in a one room hut dream of the day when the family can live in a bigger house which does not leak every time it rains. If hard-heartedness is the sin of the rich, jealousy is that of the poor. In a class-ridden society the rich oppressor has only one interest, self, and the oppressed has lost his selfhood and dignity. Thus the richest and the poorest are more beastly than the average person who has neither luxuries nor wants. An introvert is more unhappy than an extrovert, as already indicated earlier.

Deschooling and Cultural Revolution

Paulo Freire is right in listing the following myths deposited in the minds of people by the wrong educational and cultural ethos of the past which needs thorough change.

> The present oppressive order is a free society.
> All men are free to work where they want.
> They can exchange bosses if they want.
> This order respects human rights.
> Any one who is industrious can become an entrepreneur.
> The street vendor is as much an entrepreneur as the factory owner.
> There is a universal right of education.
> All men are equal in western society.
> The heroism of the oppressor class as defenders of democracy and western Christian civilisation.
> The rich are generous.
> Rebellion is a sin.
> Private property is a fundamental right.
> The rich are rich because they are industrious and the poor are poor because they are lazy.
> The poor are poor because of their natural inferiority.

He also points out, 'A revolution is achieved with neither verbalism nor activism, but rather with praxis, i.e. with reflections and action directed at the structures to be transformed'.[39] The vested interests will do everything to prevent deschooling and change which will affect the *status quo* and the interest of the dominant class. Reinhold Niebuhr has written, 'The dominant elites consider the remedy to be more domination and repression, carried out in the name of freedom, order and peace (peace of the elites, that is). Thus they can condemn logically from their point of view the violence of a strike by workers and (can) call upon the state in the same breath to use violence in putting down strike'.[40] The aim of deschooling, then, ought to be the wiping out of all such myths from the minds of the pupils by discussion, dialogue, co-investigation, and the new education needed for the creation of a classless society.

The fatalistic and docile attitude of the lowest strata of our social structures has to be removed by a cultural revolution and by new methods of education. The exploited class have no faith in themselves, no hope for the future and no sense of human dignity and worth. The educator must identify himself with them and enter into a dialogue with them. 'Dialogue further requires, to create and recreate, faith in his vocation to be more fully human (which is not the privilege of an elite alone, but the birth-right of all men). Faith in man is an *a priori* requirement for dialogue.'[41] 'I cannot think for others or without others, nor can others think for me. Even if peoples' thinking is superstitious or naive, it is only as they rethink their assumptions in action that they can change.'[42]

Though the word 'cultural revolution' has an unhealthy connotation owing to its failure in China, what Mao Tse-tung effected there should not be discarded as brain-washing. The developed countries must be ready to study the changes effected in China with an open mind and receptive heart. Something like a classless society emerged in the land of 800 million people with revolution, deschooling and cultural revolution. The gradual change that is taking place in the post-Mao China of our time may help us to penetrate beyond the bamboo curtain and see the difference between our class structure and the Chinese classless structure.

May I quote a paragraph from Dr. John Stott, one of the better evangelical theologians, who seems to have misunderstood the reference to Mao in the Bangkok Assembly of the Commission on World Mission and Evangelism of the World Council of Churches in 1973, in which I was a voting participant.

> Perhaps at no time was this confusion more evident at Bangkok than when analogies were drawn between chairman Mao and Jesus Christ. One of the documents published in preparation for the conference was entitled *Salvation Today and Contemporary Experience*. On one page someone claims to have been 'saved by Mao' while on the next someone else claims to have been saved by Jesus Christ. Similarly an American delegate said, 'Chairman Mao is God's Messiah to the Chinese', and a large poster appeared one day on the conference notice-board which, after a reference to the west's 'compulsive neurosis' to convert China, said, 'Salvation? God save China from conversion!' It may well be possible to say that Mao has 'saved' China in the sense of giving it a new national identity. But one could only say this by overlooking the appalling loss of human life and liberty by which such a national 'salvation' has been obtained. And it is childish to the point of blasphemy to

125

equate this kind of 'salvation' with the saving work of our Lord Jesus Christ.[43]

Some of us who saw the work of the kingdom of God in China through Mao and expressed it so at Bangkok were not equating Mao with Jesus Christ. Jesus Christ is the only God-man in history as the one, only, unique and absolute incarnation of the logos. Logos, being God, is the source of all goodness everywhere whether within the church or outside. It is the same logos who chose the heathen Cyrus to liberate Israel that chose Mao to liberate Chinese society from the shackles of the consumer-oriented, class-structured, exploitative social system. Wherever there is any salvation, the logos is at work and logos is identical with Jesus Christ. The criterion and source of salvation, however, is the incarnate Lord alone and not Mao. Christ has all principalities and powers (including Maoism) under his feet (Col. 1: 15-20). Mao then is not equal to Christ, but an instrument of the logos-Christ to bring about a classless society at least in one country and the Holy Spirit is at work to bring it about in the whole world through other Cyruses or Maos or Gutierrezes or Wesleys.

Cultural revolution should be aimed at without the 'appalling loss of human life'. Peaceful transition is always better than bloody revolution. In a world of sin, unfortunately, loss of human life is taking place every day through oppression, wars, exploitation, sickness, hunger, over-eating, thirst, drinking and natural calamities. The civil war or War of Independence in America also had loss of life. We can avoid the loss of life in a third world war if the resources of the world are shared by the people of the whole world controlled by a world government.

Political Party and Government for Classless Society

It is difficult to have a classless church in a class-structured society. The community in which the church is placed has unfortunately a greater influence on the church than the church has on society, especially in countries where the church is a minority. Therefore, political action is unavoidable for the

126

church to change the society. The church should teach her faithful to take a definite stand for socialism and also to encourage the party that stands for human brotherhood and liberty. The church, as a church, however, cannot identify herself with one political party because that would be encroaching on the freedom of the individual to vote for the party with which he or she has ideological agreement. The Hon. Michael Manley, Prime Minister of Jamaica since 1972, rightly told the 7th plenary meeting at the W.C.C. Nairobi Assembly that, 'Whereas the churches must first be concerned with Christian witness as it relates to personal salvation, they have also an historical mission to assist in the definition, validation, and articulation of just political, economic, and social objectives'.[44] He also pleaded for an international economic order for which also governmental action is indispensable.

It was usual in the past to say that democracy is possible because of the dignity of man and that it must be parliamentary democracy owing to the frailty of man. But parliamentary democracy has not delivered the goods it was expected to deliver in the developing countries and so most of them have now opted for other systems. It is doubtful whether the state capitalism of some of the communist countries or the parliamentary democracy of the United States will remain unaffected in the future.

Change and decay are all around us. Even parliamentary democracy is undergoing gradual change in a world of rapid social and political changes. The future is for the type of democracy that will stand for a classless society of equality of opportunity, though not equality of possessions. This is because those who work for it work with God and in accordance with the plan of God. Atheism is a negative philosophy which will not last for long even if the governments support it. The so-called people's democracy of the communist countries is also undergoing gradual change because nothing in history can remain unchanged for long.

The government of the future must itself be a proletarian government, though not the dictatorship of the proletariat. The life style of the ministers must be simple. The days of royalty are over, but ministers in many countries are outdoing and out-spending the kings of yesterday. The word minister means servant, but governmental ministers do not often think that they are servants of the people who elected them to authority. The ruler should think of himself more as a father of his subjects than ruler or judge. The church which is the servant church of the servant Christ can pave the way for the community with fraternal and filial relationships. The responsible society of tomorrow must give the responsibility to the motivated villagers and local communities rather than rule from above.

11
MISSION FOR A CLASSLESS SOCIETY

Mission is the flow of eternal love in the very being of the triune God. The incarnation was the overflow of the same agape into the historical order as the mission of God to man through the God-man. The church, as the continuation of the incarnation, must aim at the reconciliation of humanity to God and to each other and to nature. Therefore the creation of a classless society is in very nature an *esse* of mission. The new word for mission then is not just development, but the creation of a world family of humanity, aided by a trinitarian theology on the one hand and the world government on the other. *Theosis* or divinization, which is the aim of mission, worship and Christian service to the world, is primarily the creation of a world family in tune with God, fellowman and nature. Political liberation, economic justice, international economic order, cultural renewal, social transformation, world outlook are all part of the spiritualization at which the Christian mission aims in the world.

What happened to the Christian church and the Roman Empire with the Edict of Milan in 313 AD was not an unadulterated blessing, but a mixed bag of Romanization of the church and the Christianization of the Roman Empire. Today we are on the threshold of a new era in Christian mission. We are not interested in any Roman Empire any more. Our interest is mission in one world, the creation of one world, one world government, the sharing of all the resources of the whole world for the total human population. The commission of the risen Christ, 'Go ye into all the world . . .' starts with the neighbourhood of each Christian, wherever he is placed by the providence of God. The mission allotted to him includes the sharing of medicine, education, wealth, resouces and know-how. The mission of God in history is the only model for mission today. He emptied himself, took the

129

form of a servant, identified himself with the sufferings of humanity without identifying with the sin of man and created a church which was a classless society in the day of Pentecost.

Saving the Individual and the World

Mission in the past was primarily concerned with saving individuals and not with changing the structures of injustice in the world. It is necessary to redeem the person, but it must be made lasting by creating a sustainable world community. The conversion of the cannibals of the Fiji islands by the missionary activities of John Hunt and others created a new society where cannibalism was not practised. But today, there are many so-called converted Christians in the class-structured exploitative society of ours where the exploitation of the poor by the rich continues without any marked change. If conversion to Christ means the Christianization of the conscience of the converted person, how can such a person rest in peace in a capitalistic system which has not yet found a way of uniting the employer and the employee in one class of equality of opportunity? The failures of the missionary enterprises of the past such as paternalism, casteism, exclusiveness, deculturization mission-compound mentality, lack of appreciation of indigenous cultures and religions, lack of identification with the sufferings of the masses, indifference to the structural injustices of the country where mission was practised etc. were due to the pre-occupation with the concern for individual conversion without a commitment to save the world as our Lord came to do.

The gospel is a catalyst. It changes the things that it touches without a radical change in itself. As the catalyst accelerates chemical change around itself, the gospel must be allowed to change the person and the society, the community and the nation, the ruler and the ruled, the people and the governments of the world. The gospel of Jesus Christ had something to do with the Renaissance, the Reformation, the French Revolution, the American War of Independence, the Enlightenment, the abolition of slavery and *sati,* the socialist movements of the world and even the Russian Revolution.

130

The modern religious movements of India have come into being as counter-reformation in Hinduism and we must be grateful for them. The League of Nations and the United Nations took shape after a number of world missionary agencies had united the world into some sort of a world unity. Just as Raymond Panikkar speaks of *The Unknown Christ of Hinduism,* we can speak of the unknown Christ of Islam, Sikhism, Buddhism, Jainism, communism, capitalism, socialism, science, technology, the United Nations etc. since the influence of Christ knows no bounds.

Metropolitan Paulos Mar Gregorios, in an article entitled 'The Quest for the Human', has justified revolution in countries like Du Valier's Haiti. He says, 'It is in such countries where the degree of endemic or systemic violence is so high and the possibilities of constitutional change so low as clear for example in Du Valier's Haiti—that revolutions can be justified. If one fails to support revolution in such a case on the grounds of convictions of non-violence, then one is supporting the endemic or systemic violence in *status quo* which is destroying the life and dignity of man'.[45] While the 12 apostles were changed by the touch of Christ, they went around the world and the onlookers shouted, 'Those who have turned the world upside down have come here also'. Mission is the penetration of love, justice and holiness into the fabric of the individual and the society. If a light is lit in a dark room, the whole room will be illuminated though some corners hidden by barriers may not get the full light. The incarnation has brought the light to the whole world and it is our duty to remove the human barriers that prevent the light of the gospel from penetration to every area. It is the recalcitrant man who hides the light of God because of his selfishness. Therefore the conversion of the person is important. But that is not enough. Just as the health of a new-born baby is dependent on the health of the mother or the nurse, the new life of the Christian depends on the new life of the church and the world. This is the reason why we ought to evolve a comprehensive mission and theory of mission oriented towards a classless society.

131

Mission as Sarvodaya

The title of John Ruskin's book *Unto This Last* borrowed from our Lord's lips as recorded in the parable of those who were hired at various hours and paid equally (Matt. 20), was translated as *Sarvodaya* (Development of All) by Mahatma Gandhi. We ought to praise God for the Sarvodaya movement in India as everything good comes from God, and as Christ is God, from Christ. The ideology of Sarvodaya is in line with the theology of a classless society. Christian mission must not aim at the development of any one nation or people, but of the whole people of the whole world. He who worked for 6 hours should not grudge or complain when he who worked only for 1 hour is also paid the same. God who is the driving force of all missionaries, cannot reward on the basis of work alone, but as he is the Father of all, must look into the need also. The one who was ready to work for 6 hours, but got the job only for 1 hour had certain basic needs to be met. Therefore, he must also be paid the basic salary.

The parable of the 5 talents (Matt. 25; Luke 19), on the other hand, is to point out the danger of idleness and the need of giving incentive to those who work extremely hard. In each of these parables, the owner is God and not man. 'Am I not allowed to do what I choose with what belongs to me?' is the question that God alone has the right to ask. The proprietor, the so-called owner, the capitalist, the feudal lord, the estate owner, the managing director etc. are all God's employees and not owners of the resources of God. God wants to pay all of them on the basis of their work and need and not on the basis of status or education or rank. God who planted the garden of Eden and created the world and all things visible and invisible is the only owner in the right sense of the word. If Adam had been given the ownership of the garden of Eden, he could not have been expelled from it. Therefore, 'the Lord God took the man and put him in the garden of Eden to till it and to keep it'. Every created being is given a mission to humanity at large. No ideal father of a family will want his own prosperity without that of other members of his family. Similarly, no citizen of a country should be concerned about the well-being of his own family without that of the neighbour's family.

Mission that aims at *sarvodaya,* or welfare of all, is aware of the fact that God has not created resources to make every person a millionaire and there is no need for it. Scientists, more than missionaries, have acutely felt the danger of energy crisis, oil crisis, water-shortage, mineral crisis etc. in our time. They are asking for zero point development in the rich countries and a sacramental attitude to nature. The rich will not be able to go forward leaving the poor behind for the latter will overthrow them somehow or other. The weapon of collective bargaining hidden in strikes has convinced the employer that if the employees are left trailing behind, they will not be able to make any headway.

The twin commandments to love God perfectly and our neighbour as ourself (Luke 10:27) contain the whole theology of a classless society and the mission for *sarvodaya*. The neighbour is not necessarily a Christian. Any man in need, whether Jew or Samaritan, has to be regarded as a neighbour, but we become a neighbour only when we act like the Good Samaritan. The mission of the Good Samaritan was to make the wounded brother as healthy as himself and to spend every ounce of energy and resources for that purpose. The wine, the oil, the ass, the money and the time he possessed and earned later were all spent for mission for *sarvodaya*. Unlike the priest and the Levite who passed by without a missionary passion, perhaps in their over-enthusiasm to perform the rites in the temple correctly at the right time, the Good Samaritan showed not only love, but also justice by sharing all his earnings with his neighbour.

The question remains whether a peaceful transformation of society would take place in the world as Indian *sarvodaya* envisages. As the barley cake which tumbled into the camp of Midian and lay flat the enemy's tent (Judges 7:13) the Christian mission of Christ has a hidden potentiality to overthrow the citadels of the oppressor and the enemy and create an egalitarian society in the fullness of time. Let us pray and work for it.

Mission Tomorrow

I am writing this chapter in a Christian rest house among the

133

tea gardens of Munnar, Kerala. Millions of tea plants which are pruned to size grow happily here serving humanity around the world by supplying delicious tea for the thirsty. The hillsides looking like green tea carpets are given shade by certain tall shade trees but the tea plants are not allowed to grow taller than their neighbours. Their only desire is to live long and serve humanity and not to grow taller than their brothers. The choice for man tomorrow is whether to grow tall and live only for a short time like the shade trees or to be short but live long like a tea plant that allows others to pluck its buds as long as it lives. Certainly a tea garden is a beautiful site, more exquisite than even the green paddy fields which live only for a short time. The shade trees serve the tea plants and the tea plants serve humanity. When it comes to the human side, however, the owners of these gardens grow tall and serve themselves without serving the tea pluckers and the labourers who are pruned to size by them lest they grow strong and catch up with them. The daily wage of the tea pluckers remains 5 rupees normally even now when the price of tea has jumped up to 30 rupees per kilogram. This is the dangerous class-structured society of the rich employer and the poor employee which must be changed as early as possible. Why can't they share the profit with the employees?

Mission tomorrow, then, must aim at breaking all middle walls of partition which separate the lord and the slave, the rich and the poor, the oppressor and the oppressed, the highly paid and the unemployed, those who live in huge houses and those who have nowhere to lay their heads, the luxurious and the needy. The missionaries must not only preach the gospel of human brotherhood under the Fatherhood of God, but must also practise a simpler life style. All Christians who have huge incomes must be taught that it is a sin to keep their income for their own families alone without giving employment opportunities to the unemployed of their neighbourhood. In the parable of Dives and Lazarus, the sin of the rich man was that he remained rich when his neighbour was poor and needy.

It is unfortunate that no one in the ecumenical meetings raises a hue and cry against the inter-communion of the rich and the poor around the same table of the Lord as did St. Paul in 1 Corinthians 11: 20. 'When you meet together, it is not the Lord's supper that you eat. For in eating each one goes ahead with his own meal, and one is hungry and another is drunk'. The Orthodox Churches do not inter-commune on account of the distance in the ecclesiology and sacramental theology of the churches. There is a sound scriptural basis for someone who will not inter-commune until there is an international economic order and sharing of all the resources of the rich with the poor. The early church shared in the communion table only after sharing the material riches with their fellow-believers (Acts 2:44–48). Dietrich Bonhoeffer, though a liberal, was orthodox in pointing his accusing finger at the theory of 'cheap grace' practised by churches and Christians.

The Bangkok Conference of the Commission on World Mission and Evangelism in 1973 declared, 'Mission in 6 continents (declared at Mexico) has ended, mission in one world has started'. The aim of mission cannot be anything less than the deification, unification and reconciliation of all churches and the whole world into the unity of the measure and the stature of the fulness of Christ.

APPENDIX 1

YOUR QUERIES ANSWERED

1. Is not the phrase 'classless society' communist and so un-Christian?

Language is universal and not communist or capitalist. The idea behind the classless society is basically based on the Bible and Christian theology. The first expression of it was in the Jerusalem community soon after Pentecost. If Karl Marx used it and popularized it with a technical meaning of its own, this does not mean that others should not use it. It is a powerful phrase and if it has any materialistic meaning, we can purge it and use it in the Christian sense. When 'the whole body of believers was united in heart and soul and not a man of them claimed any of his possessions as his own' it was certainly a classless society. They held everything in common. The time has come for the world also to hold everything in common and so the time is ripe for the theology of a classless society.

2. Why did the sharing experiment of the Jerusalem community fail?

There were at least 3 reasons for it. First, they expected the imminent return of the Lord and so did not start common production. It is clear that common consumption without common production is bound to fail. Second, there was a slow backsliding of the Christians owing to the selfishness of people like Ananias and Sapphira, who sold everything but brought only a part of it to the apostles for common use. Third, the death of Ananias and Sapphira must have created a fear complex and the love of God and fellowmen waned in such an atmosphere. The passage ends with the statement, 'great fear came upon the whole church, and upon all who heard of these things' (Acts 5:11).

3. *How do you know that the new classless society you desire will not fail?*

A patient is treated for his illness without any guarantee that he or she will not become ill again. We know that the class-structured society of our time is unhealthy and needs treatment. We must take all precautions lest the illness should recur. The world government, national units of the world government, education for a classless society, a new cultural revolution which is not brain-washing, sharing communities at local levels, lack of opportunities to invest black money, priority on the basic needs of man, discouraging the productions of luxury items, a proletarian life style from top to bottom etc. would help to perpetuate the health created by the classless society.

4. *Will it not be too monotonous as the present life style of China?*

Monotony can be reduced if the technological and scientific know-how of the developed countries is put to the service of the new society. A classless society of the whole world will include all the multifarious peoples of the whole world with their various artistic, cultural riches and varieties. The expenses of the bourgeois life style of the small minority can be used for building houses for the homeless majority of the world in different sustainable patterns. The luxury of the few can be invested for the necessity of many. The Chinese monotonous life style is due to the pressurized and pulverized society created there by the Maoist revolution. The new classless society brought about freely from the bottom and democratically from the top need not be so monotonous.

5. *Does the classless society mean equality in everything?*

Certainly not. The pattern of the body and organs given by St. Paul is to be followed.

> For just as in a single human body there are many limbs and organs, all with different functions, so all of us, united with Christ, form one body, serving individually as limbs and organs to one another (Rom. 12: 4).
>
> For the body does not consist of one member but of many. If the foot should say, 'Because I am not a hand, I do not belong to the body', that would not make it any less a part of the body . . . On

the contrary, the parts of the body which seem to be weaker are indispensable . . . But God has so adjusted the body, giving the greater honour to the inferior part, that there may be no discord in the body, but that the members may have the same care for one another. If one member suffers all suffer together; if one member is honoured all rejoice together (1 Cor. 12:12-26).

In the body the equality is in the opportunity to grow together and not in functions. The heart pumps blood to all parts of the body and all sections of the body are connected to the brain by the central nervous system. There is no isolated existence for anyone, but all exist for one another and all grow together in solidarity.

6. What is wrong with the American way of life? Is it not a classless society?

No capitalistic country including the United States has solved the problem of unemployment. Education is becoming more and more expensive as is medical treatment. The lowest strata cannot have the same treatment as the highest strata of society. The integration of the whites and the coloured has not taken place as the Brahmins and Harijans are not integrated in India. The luxurious life style of a few millionaires is unpardonable if we take the stewardship of wealth as a Christian ideal to measure with. There is poverty in the midst of plenty even in the United States. The East Harlem of New York is an example.

7. What is wrong with the Indian society on this point?

The distance between the rich and the poor is even greater in India than in the United States. 85 families own nearly 40% of the wealth of India. 60% of Indians still live below the poverty line. India has to feed 18% of the population of the world in 2½% of the area of the world with 1½% of the wealth of the world. The percentage of the landless had increased during the past 25 years of independence. The rich are getting richer and the poor poorer in India also. India does not have anything like the bare-footed doctors of China for the teeming millions in the villages. The powerless at the bottom do not even realize the hidden power in their hands, though in the recent election (1977) they used the ballot box to overthrow the government.

139

India can never progress without a classless society, though the road is long and tedious.

8. *Is not the theology of a classless society impracticable and utopian?*

Was not Jesus Christ impracticable and utopian when he taught, 'Be ye therefore perfect as your heavenly Father is perfect' (Matt. 5: 48)? Is the twin commandment about loving God 'with all your heart and all your soul, and with all your strength, and with all your mind; and your neighbour as yourself' (Luke 10: 27) practicable? Even communism has set a utopian hope before its adherents. The goal set before us must always be idealistic and perfect. It is our sin and selfishness that attack the ideal of a classless and brotherly social order. Vested interest will not only put new hurdles in its way, but try to thwart it by every ounce of its energy. But those who believe in God should not be pessimistic and frustrated. Our duty is to aim at the will of God and let God use us for achieving it. We must trust in the promise of God, 'With God all things are possible'.

9. *Is not the church the most class-structured society in the world?*

I have to give a paradoxical answer for this. It is both the most class-structured and at the same time most classless society in the world because it contains both types. There are innumerable sharing classless communities in the church and yet the class distinctions are quite marked in the life style of the members of the church in many countries. The popes, patriarchs, bishops, district superintendents etc. have lived like kings and emperors of the past. The truth is that if the society is classful the church is classful and if the society is classless the church is classless. The life style of the popes of Rome became luxurious because of the life style of the emperors of the Roman Empire whom the popes used to consecrate. The Christian Czars of Russia saw to it that the patriarchs lived in palaces. The marriage of church and state made the church classful. Now, with the disappearance of royalty from most of the countries of the world, the church can move towards a classless society and a simpler life style.

10. Can the hierarchical structure of the church be fitted into the new society?

As already pointed out in chapter 4, the pyramidical hierarchy has to give way to the trinitarian hierarchy and collegiality. Monarchical hierarchy developed in the church only from the 2nd century and the international head in the person of the pope is not the gift of the Holy Spirit, but that of the Roman Empire. In the New Testament each church is a full manifestation of the whole church. The Church was one, holy, catholic and apostolic only when it was in Jerusalem. When questions of dispute arose, it was the Jerusalem Council that settled it and not James alone or Peter alone. The key sentence of authority in the church is 'It seemed good to the Holy Spirit and to us'. The veto power of the Roman pope, which is the vestige of royalty and the sign of pyramidical hierarchy, has to give way to the authority of the ecumenical councils, when need arises, to decide on a question that affects all. The Holy Spirit is leading the church to the full truth of Trinity at every level including that of papacy and so a democratic hierarchy is not an impossibility.

11. How would you unite the Catholic substance, Protestant principle and the Orthodox ethos into the theology of a classless society?

Paul Tillich spoke only of the first two, but I am adding the third as there is a trinitarian principle here also. The reunited Christendom will be neither Roman Catholic nor Protestant, but the manifestation of the body of Christ. None of the three branches of Christendom should regard the two other branches as second-class citizens, but respect them as brothers in Christ. The triune God is present in each and in all and the dialogue for reunion must be on the basis of equality and not with any superiority complex on the part of any. There should be an inter-penetration of the emphasis of each to the other confessions. It is sometimes pointed out that the Roman Catholic Church has the Father image, the Protestant the Christological centrality and the Orthodox the Pneumatical stress. The union of Christendom must be organic and not federal as God is absolutely one in three and three in one. Peter, James and John at the top will be co–equal with the role of first among equals for the successor of Peter. But all decisions will be unanimous and collegial, guided by the Holy Spirit. It will be the decisions of the whole apostolic college that will be declared by the Father, Peter. The seven 'ones' of Ephesians 4:4f. must be experienced in the united church.

12. Is there any place for dissent or individual freedom in the classless society?

As we are not God, but human beings, differences of opinion are bound to come and that is necessary, but the truth will finally emerge as unanimous. The Quakers or the Society of Friends have been practising this now for a long time. As governments cannot be expected to wait upon the Lord patiently till unanimity is arrived at, majority decisions may have to be sought after and implemented. Once a government is elected on the basis of democratic procedures, the elected government must care for the welfare of all including those who voted against them, as all belong to one class of citizens. •

13. If all agree on the theology of a classless society, why should there be an opposition party and parliamentary democracy? Is not one party enough?

'New brooms sweep clean.' Any party may get tired or corrupted and so the opposition party must be there to give correction to those in power or to vote them out if they are corrupt. Every human being is 'a mighty man of valour, but a leper'. The fallibility of man makes it necessary that he does not take it for granted that his powers will always be with him. Almost all autocrats of history have become demonic in the long run. It is when the rulers act against the classless society that they must be voted out by the majority and the reins of government given to the opposition party.

14. If the church is one class, are not the non-Christians of another class?

Not at all. Humanity at large is one class on the basis of the common image of God given in creation. None should be discriminated against as of another class on the basis of religious affiliation. The Good Samaritan did not consider the wounded traveller Jew as of another class. Though Joseph

142

showed special concern about Benjamin because both were of the same mother, Rachel, Christians must be able to treat Reubens and Benjamins alike as both are sons of one father. The sun gives light to good and bad objects in the same manner. Love and concern must become our second nature to be expressed to all of humanity, Christians or non–Christians. Social services should never become a bait to hook non-Christians to the church. We must love others because we are loved. Christ loved us while we were sinners. He healed the daughter of the heathen Syrophoenician woman as much as the mother-in-law of Peter. He was perhaps the first Jew to ask water of a Samaritan woman. Duty for duty's sake is taught by Bhagavadgita and Immanuel Kant and we must also practise it without having an ulterior motive in mission either.

15. *What are the points in which your view of classless society differs from the communist view?*

(a) Communism teaches economic determinism, materialism and atheism, but I teach divine providence, spiritualism and theism which is trinitarian.

(b) In the place of the dictatorship of the proletariat, I teach parliamentary democracy and out and out socialism.

(c) In communism 'the end justifies the means'. We must aim at the purification of the means also that the end may be pure. Though compromise will often be necessary, the aim of pure means should be kept in mind.

(d) Class war and bloody revolution are indispensable for communism, but the means ought to be love and law making in the Christian view of a classless society. A spiritual revolution, education for a classless society etc. will tame the class war even if it becomes the lesser of the two evils in certain societies controlled by vested interests.

(e) Communism believes in the one–party system and the so–called people's democracy, whereas I believe in parliamentary democracy.

(f) Christian love is obsolete in communism as the emphasis is on might and right. We would stress love and justice instead of might and right. There is a joy in social justice affected by love and sacrifice.

16. What are the points in which your view of classless society agrees with the communist view?

(a) There should be nationalization of the means of production,i.e. land, machinery, farm equipments etc.

(b) Education and medical aid must be made available for all with the principle of equality of opportunity for all.

(c) The present wide disparity between salaries must be done away with.

(d) Priority must be given to the production of food, clothing and other basic needs of all the citizens and not to luxury items.

(e) Construction of huge private houses should not be undertaken, but small houses or apartments should be built for all citizens and allocated on the basis of the need of the family and not on the basis of status.

(f) Jobs for all must be the aim of planning and incentive for better workers must be possible, measuring the amount of work done by each.

(g) There should be a cultural revolution, educating the people to the aim of work as nation-building and not only the welfare of one's family.

(h) A disciplined life and moral standards must be the gift of the educational system.

(i) Research and a scientific outlook should also be encouraged among the students in the educational system.

17. Why are you pessimistic about a classless society being brought about by benevolent capitalism?

Max Weber, R. H. Tawney and others have shown by research that the protestant ethic of individual freedom has been the harbinger of capitalism in the world. The achievements of capitalism have been by competition and not by co-operation. The profit-motive, which is the basis of capitalism has created an unbridgable gulf between the employer and the employed and the exploitation of the resources of nature has also reached a danger point. But for capitalism the energy crisis would not have been with us so soon. There is a difference between the profit of the state which is shared for all and the profit of the capitalist which is accumulated in a few pockets. The capitalist uses the employees as tools for their

144

profits and not as human beings with as much dignity as himself. The bungalows of the owners of the means of production and the shacks and small apartments of the employees tell the whole world that capitalism creates two distinct classes, if not more. Capitalism has not given equality of opportunity to all the citizens of any country so far. It creates artificial shortages of things which it manufactures so as to increase the price. If the capitalist begins to obey the commandment of the Lord, 'love thy neighbour as yourself' he will end up in socialism.

18. *Why can't we try mixed economy as a means of creating a classless society with freedom of the individual to join either?*

India has tried it and has not succeeded. The psychology of the mixed economy is one that would create a set of idlers in the public sector and profiteers in the private sector and thus continue the class structure. Those who work in the public sector know that they cannot make as much money as their friends in the private sector and so they do not work hard. Although the labourers in the private sector may be better paid, the profit they make goes just to the proprietor or owners. The unemployment problem will also remain in the mixed economy.

19. *Is not the classless society likely to take away the initiative from the people?*

China has disproved this fear. The Chinese work harder today than when they were in a class-structured society. Nation building has become the driving force for them to work hard. Selfishness alone is not the incentive for hard work. The initiative of Mother Teresa today and of Father Damien yesterday to suffer for others was not the profit-motive. Christianity and all the living religions of the world have the God-given duty to teach people that there is a joy in working for God and others.

APPENDIX 2

AN APOLOGIA FOR THE APPLICATION OF THE DOCTRINE OF TRINITY TO LIFE IN THIS BOOK

This book is not a treatise on the mystery of Trinity. It takes the mystery of Trinity as unknowable by human intellect in its fullness and agrees with the Fathers of the church who were unanimous in the inadequacies of analogies from the created order to explain the totality of Trinity. The Unitarians of England during the last century pointed their finger at the logical difficulty of explaining the Trinity when they said, 'If ideas are attached to the words employed, Trinitarianism is in reality either Tritheism or Sabellianism'.[46]

There is a tendency among western theologians to speak of immanent or essential Trinity which speaks of the unity of essence and of the economic Trinity which relates the threeness in the economy of salvation, but these phraseologies were foreign to the Fathers of the Eastern church. Yet Karl Rahner tries to relate the two as follows, 'The immanent Trinity is known in faith because the economic Trinity has been seen to be at work in the history of salvation. The economic Trinity is not merely the means of gaining knowledge of the immanent Trinity, but is the same thing'.[47]

It is sometimes pointed out that there is hardly a theologian whose doctrine of Trinity has not been called heretical by his opponents. The Eastern Fathers are charged with tritheism by Karl Barth and others and Barth is said to be modalist by many of his critics. W. R. Matthews says, 'It is well known that theology has made use of two classes of analogy in order to throw light upon the doctrine of the Trinity, that of the individual person and that of a society. The first of these . . . is employed by Augustine . . . the second was used by the Cappadocian Fathers . . . It now seems to me that we can go further and see that the two analogies really converge'.[48]

It is my conviction that the unity and plurality of a nuclear family is one of the best analogies to show how they converge in the Holy Trinity perfectly and in human nuclear families imperfectly. Robert S. Franks also sees the advantage of the social doctrine of Trinity over the individualistic. He says, 'It must be admitted that the social doctrine of the Trinity seems to have an advantage. Even when a timeless truth is substituted for an impossible bit of history, there still remains a sufficient distinction of the persons to justify the popular view that the Son of God "descended from heaven". Thus there is a closer approximation to creed, hymn and liturgy'.[49] Whatever then a critic of the view of Trinity in this book might point out, the approach I have taken is more in line with the patristic thought than with the Augustinian, though there is an element of novelty in it.

I may quote, however, a section from the fifth theological oration of Gregory of Nazianzus to show that the analogy I have taken is not completely new. Gregory, who was an apophatic (negative) theologian and spent a lot of his time explaining the incomprehensibility and unexpressibility of the mystery of the Godhead, uses the analogy of Adam, Eve and Seth to explain this great mystery. To quote at length,

What was Adam? A creature of God. What then was Eve? A fragment of the creature. And what was Seth? The begotten of both. Does it then seem to you that Creature and Fragment and Begotten are same thing? Of course it does not. But were not these persons consubstantial? Of course they were. Well then, here is an acknowledged fact that different persons may have the same substance. I say this not that I would attribute creation or fraction or any property of body to the Godhead (let none of your contenders for a word be down upon me again), but that I may contemplate in these as on a stage, things which are objects of thought alone. For it is not possible to trace out any image exactly to the whole extent of truth. But they say, what is the meaning of all this? For is not the one an offspring and the other a something else of the One? Did not both Eve and Seth come from the one Adam? And were they both begotten by him? No: but one was a fragment of him and the other was begotten by him. And yet the

148

two were one and the same thing; both were human beings; no one will deny that. Will you then give up your contention against the Spirit, that he must be either altogether begotten, or else cannot be consubstantial, or be God; and admit from human examples the possibility of our position? I think it will be well for you unless you are determined to be very quarrelsome and to fight against what is proved to demonstration.[50]

Furthermore, to the Orthodox theologians of the 4th century, the logos was not impersonal but personal. The logos is eternally personal. In the third theological oration Gregory of Nazianzus says, 'He who is now man, was once uncompounded. What he was he continued to be; what he was not he took to himself'.[51] Robert S. Franks comments, 'It could not be more clearly or succinctly stated that the logos is the personal element in the incarnation; and this is the view of all the Orthodox Fathers'.

The patristic definition of the Trinity as one substance and three persons is too philosophical to be understood by ordinary people, but the definition 'one family and three persons' means the same thing and can be understood even by the child in spite of the danger of age differences in earthly families. This risk can be slightly overcome by telling the student that everything in the Godhead is eternal as he is the same yesterday, today and for ever. Eternal fatherhood implies eternal sonship and eternal motherhood for none without a child is a father or a mother. Linguistic limitation is there in everything we speak about God. The arguments of St. Athanasius for the co-eternity of the logos with the Father are equally applicable to the co-eternity of the Son with the Father. As there is no fire or sun without light and heat, there is no Father without the Son and the Spirit.

Again, in an ideal nuclear family, all the activities are in unity and solidarity. As Gregory of Nyssa writes (*non tres dei*), 'The Father never acts independently of the Son, nor the Son of the Spirit'.[52] The point that Nyssa makes about the lack of solidarity among the human race cannot be said about the loving nuclear family. G. L. Prestige writes:

Gregory of Nyssa is in a position to state that the Father is God and Son is God; but this assertion does not preclude the truth that God is one, because in the Godhead there can be discerned no

149

difference, either in nature or operation . . . In man he says, in spite of solidarity of the whole race, each individual acts separately, so that it is proper to regard them as many; each is separated into an individual unity by the fact of the independence of the 'energy'. This is not so, he proceeds with God.[53]

My argument in this book is that there is a lack of solidarity among fallen humanity on account of sin and that redemption is reconciliation with God and man in the model of the Holy Trinity leading ultimately to a classless society. The perfect ideal is not attainable in the historical order, but still the ideal must always be kept before us as the command is 'Be ye therefore perfect even as your heavenly Father is perfect'. The ontological gulf between God and man which is stressed by Karl Barth and others is only a half truth. The Fathers taught *theosis* which means, 'when he appears we shall be like him' (1 John 3:2). 'Gregory of Nazianzus (Or. 31:16) maintains in a memorable sentence that each of the divine persons possesses a unity with the associate persons, no less actual than with himself, by reason of the identity of *ousia* and of power; and this is the ground of the divine unity'.[54] Is this not the ground of human unity also?

The Fathers are right in pointing out again and again that the Holy Trinity is to be worshipped and not scrutinized. The whole depth and height of the doctrine is not seen by any human ingenuity. But the adorable Godhead is also to be emulated. The God whom we worship is also the God whom we follow to the uttermost. His image in us is in the trichotomy of body, mind and soul or *soma, nous* and *psyche* as well as in the triad of the family. The relevance of God in life is both personal and social. Anything approximating to perfection in history is trinitarian and not unitarian or binitarian (eg. in one dialectic there is thesis, antithesis and synthesis; in one time, past, present and future; in one water, vapour, water and ice; in one person in grammar, first person, second person and third person; in one concrete reality, matter, liquid and ether; in one mind, unconscious mind, preconscious mind and conscious mind etc.). Similarly, any family which is binitarian is not a perfect family. Thus, we have many insights into the Trinity even in the created order, though God the triune is beyond all these analogies.

150

Karl Rahner rightly points out that 'The whole economy of salvation has a trinitarian structure'.[55] He refers to Schmaus who makes 'theology of the Trinity the basic structural principle of the whole treatise *De Deo'*, and asks whether one should combine 'the doctrine of the nature of God with that of God in three persons, as has been done once more recently by Schmaus'?[56] As an Indian Christian who is surrounded by the basic thought pattern of *Advaita* which identifies the individual self with the supreme self, I believe that the Christian doctrine of *imago Dei* has to be interpreted emphatically as the image of the triune God in the family as well as in each member of the family in the sense that the triune God is perfect God, God the Father is perfect God, the Son is perfect God and the Holy Spirit is perfect God, and yet there are not three Gods but one God.

The image of God in the family of Adam, Eve and Seth has been ignored for a long time by Christian theologians. God the logos is not illogical. He needs triune existence in all eternity for his eternal love to be in eternal action with the only three elements of giving, receiving and sharing. He was not a monad without active love before the creation of angels or persons. His love is so perfect that he is both three persons and one person at the same time just as three persons in one family.

J. R. Illingworth at the beginning of this century wrote that the creed is not an intellectual explanation, but a living experience. To quote,

> For how is it that we really come into immediate contact with the Christian Creed in our own experience in the present day? Not primarily as a living and breathing and organized society of men and women all round us, whose creed is only the intellectual explanation of their actual life. And that actual life consists in the conviction of those who are sincerely living it, in progressive communion with the Father, through fellowship in the mystical body of his Son, effected by the operation of the Holy Spirit within them.[57]

My own contention is that when we manifest the classless society in history in the power and imitation of the Holy Trinity, Christian theology will become more relevant than ever before. There is no theology in Christianity which is not a systematic explanation of the person and work of the Holy

Trinity. Therefore the theology of the classless society must be based on the Trinity. Raymond Panikkar agrees when he writes that 'in reality the Trinity is not only the theoretical foundation stone of Christianity, but also the practical concrete, existential basis of the Christian life'.[58]

Coming to the Faith and Order Study on 'What Unity Requires?' the conciliar fellowship envisaged is also on the trinitarian model. The Nairobi Assembly of the World Council of Churches has approved the insight that 'True conciliarity is the reflection in the life of the church of the triune being of God. It is that unity for which Christ prayed when he asked the Father that his disciples might be one *as* the Father and the Son are one'.[59] The connection between unity and diversity is also related to the Holy Trinity in the report. 'It is because the unity of the church is grounded in the divine triunity that we can speak of diversity in the church as something to be not only admitted but actively desired. Since Christ died and rose for all and his church is to be the sign of the coming unity of humankind, it must be open to women and men of every nation and culture, of every time and place, of every sort of ability and disability'.[60]

The final authority on which the theology of a classless society is based is the high priestly prayer of our Lord himself recorded in St. John 17.

> I do not pray for these only, but also for those who believe in me through their word, that they may all be one; even as thou, Father, art in me, and I in thee, that they also may be in us, so that the world may believe that thou hast sent me. The glory which thou hast given me I have given to them, that they may be one even as we are one, I in them and thou in me, that they may become perfectly one, so that the world may know that thou hast sent me and hast loved them even as thou has loved me.

NOTES

1. Quoted by C. T. Kurian, *Poverty and Development,* C.L.S. Madras 1974, p. 3.
2. Ibid. p. 7.
3. *Indian Express,* 18th April 1977.
4. Ibid.
5. SPAN, May 1977, pp. 2-4.
6. *Indian Express,* 19th April 1977
7. Ibid. 25th April 1977.
8. Frederick Herzog, 'Birth Pangs: Liberation Theology in North America', in *The Christian Century,* 15th December 1976, p. 1120. Reprinted by permission.
9. Ibid. p. 1121.
10. Ibid. p. 1122, quoting Glenn R. Bucher, *Straight/White/ Male,* Fortress Press 1976.
11. SPAN, May 1977, p. 4.
12. Ibid.
13. *International Review of Mission,* World Council of Churches, July 1975, p. 267.
14. John Gerassi (ed.), *Camilo Torres: Revolutionary Priest,* Random House, Inc. and Brandt & Brandt, p. 322. Reproduced by permission.
15. Ibid. p. 323
16. Ibid. p. 324
17. Leslie Dewart, *The Future of Belief,* London 1967, p. 49.
18. *Revolutionary Priest,* op. cit., p. 321.
19. 'Amongst all the terrible disasters of the Black Death when it seemed that God was behaving like a lion, a great woman of prayer, Julian of Norwich, concluded that though she had been taught God could be angry this was a mistake. Though he is almighty yet he loves like a woman, like a mother.' Bible Reading Fellowship Notes, 31st June 1977.

20. Hans Küng, *Christ sein*, R. Piper & Co. Verlag 1974, pp. 466f. (E. Tr. *On Being a Christian*, Wm. Collins 1977.)

21. F. L. Cross and E. A. Livingstone (eds.), *The Oxford Dictionary of the Christian Church* (2nd edition), Oxford University Press 1974, p. 93.

22. Quoted by Stephen Eagie in SPAN, June 1977, p. 11.

23. C. T. Kurian, *Poverty and Development*, C.L.S. Madras 1974, p. 31f.

24. *Nicene and Post Nicene Fathers, Series II*, Vol. VIII, p. 116.

25. Ibid. Section 44, p. 28.

26. V. Lossky, *The Mystical Theology of the Eastern Church*, James Clarke & Co. Ltd. 1957, p. 174.

27. Ibid. p. 176.

28. J. Meyendorff, *The Orthodox Church*, Darton, Longman & Todd 1962, p. 192.

29. Quoted by Robin Boyd, *An Introduction to Indian Christian Theology*, C.L.S. Madras 1969, p. 106

30. Karl Rahner, *Studies in Modern Theology*, Burns & Oates Ltd. 1965, p. 195.

31. Ibid, p. 201.

32. Alexander Schmemann, *Historical Road of Eastern Orthodoxy*, Harvill Press Ltd. 1963, p. 16.

33. *The Guardian*, Madras, 15th August 1976.

34. Ibid.

35. P. Freire, *The Pedagogy of the Oppressed*, Sheed & Ward 1973 and Seabury Press. Reprinted by permission.

36. P. Freire, *Cultural Action for Freedom*, Penguin Books 1974. P. Freire, *Education for Critical Consciousness*, Sheed & Ward 1974.

37. H. Camara, 'The Peaceful Overthrow of the Structure of Slavery', in *Idea and Action Bulletin*, Vol. I, 1972.

38. See *The Pedagogy of the Oppressed*, p. 109.

39. Ibid. p. 96.

40. R. Niebuhr, *Moral Man and Immoral Society*, Scribner 1960, p. 51.

41. Ibid. p. 63.

42. Ibid. p. 80.

43. J. R. W. Stott, *Christian Mission in the Modern World*, Falcon Press 1975, pp. 95f. Reproduced by permission.

44. D. M. Paton (ed.), *Breaking Barriers, Nairobi 1975,* S.P.C.K. and Eerdmans 1976, p. 22.
45. Paulos Mar Gregorios, 'The Quest for the Human', *Quest for Certainty,* Orthodox Seminary Kottayam 1976.
46. Leonard Hodgson, *The Doctrine of the Trinity,* James Nisbet & Co. Ltd. 1960, p. 219.
47. Karl Rahner (ed.), *Sacramentum Mundi,* Vol. VI, Burns & Oates Ltd. 1970, p. 305.
48. W. R. Matthews, *God in Christian Thought and Experience,* James Nisbet & Co. Ltd. 1930, p. 193.
49. Robert S. Franks, *The Doctrine of Trinity,* Gerald Duckworth & Co. Ltd. 1953, p. 200.
50. Five Orations of Gregory of Nazianzus, V. II.
51. Ibid. V. III.19.
52. J. P. Minge (ed.), Gregory of Nyssa, *Patrologia Latina,* Paris 1844–65, Vol. 35, 133A.
53. G. L. Prestige, *God in Patristic Thought,* S.P.C.K. 1975, p. 260. Reproduced by permission.
54. Ibid. p. 261.
55. Karl Rahner (ed.), *Sacramentum Mundi*, Vol. VI, Burns & Oates Ltd. 1970, p. 304.
56. Ibid. p. 303.
57. J. R. Illingworth, *The Doctrine of Trinity,* Macmillan 1907, p. 150.
58. Raymond Panikkar, *Trinity and World Religions,* C.L.S. Madras 1970, p. 42.
59. World Council of Churches, Faith and Order Paper No. 77, p. 65.
60. Ibid. p. 66.

INDEX

157

158